FOOTBRIDGE TO ENCHANTMENT

Articles from Nigel Tranter's country notebook first appeared in *The Scots Magazine* in 1962. This illustrated collection brings them together for the first time in paperback.

All Nigel Tranter's novels have been written on walks which start on the long timber footbridge that leads to Aberlady Bay, and his autobiographical country notebook is a marvellous evocation of the landscape that has inspired him. In *Footbridge to Enchantment* the bay, with its tides ebbing and flowing over the mudflats, and its saltings and dune country frequented by waders, terns, eiders and sand martins, forms a backdrop for the author's inimitable recounting of his experiences over the years.

Although the original bridge was demolished by a storm in February 1990, it has now been replaced and in its new form is still crossed daily by Nigel Tranter.

Nigel Tranter's writing career spans more than half a century and he is the author of over eighty novels, as well as numerous works of non-fiction. His first novel, *Trespass*, was published in 1935, and after service in the Second World War he became a full time writer. His best-selling novels include *The Bruce Trilogy*, *Balefire* and *The Gilded Fleece*.

NIGEL TRANTER'S COUNTRY NOTEBOOK

FOOTBRIDGE TO ENCHANTMENT

EDINBURGH
B&W PUBLISHING
1993

First published 1992
This Edition published 1993
by B&W Publishing
Edinburgh
ISBN 1 873631 23 5

British Library Cataloguing in Publication Data:
A catalogue record for this book is available from
the British Library

Cover photograph by Donald Clements
Illustrations by Colin Gibson
Cover design Harry Palmer

Printed by Biddles Ltd, Guildford

Contents

Preface

The following observations, reflections and anecdotes, were
made over a considerable number of years; and nothing is
more true than that conditions and circumstances change,
natural as well as human ones – even in such as myself; and the
latter can affect the former, and have done so in Aberlady Bay.
As an example, the vast increase in the amount of plastic found
necessary to sustain life in our variety of civilisation, and the
distressingly durable qualities of the same. The problem has
grown excessively. Plastics, in the form of containers, cartons,
tubes, bags and sheeting, get washed up on the bar and
beaches, presumably coming from rubbish dumps up and
down the Firth of Forth. They lie, not mouldering away as do
seaweeds, wood and the like, and catch the blown sand, a
permanent feature of the bay, to form little hills on which
marram-grass seeds implant themselves, to catch still more
sand and grow into new dunes – this at a vastly increased rate
than heretofore. So the dune-country is extending westwards
most notably, and in consequence, the bay's width lessening.
In another twenty years...?

This is just one development. Another is the increasing use
by the public of the Nature Reserve, as it becomes ever better-
known and appreciated, especially by birdwatchers of course
– and that hobby has made great advances in recent years –
but also just by walkers from Edinburgh and elsewhere, and by
sun-and-sand worshippers of various sorts. All to the good, to
be sure; but some effects on the environment are inevitable.
Whether this is in any way responsible for the disappearance
of hares, which used to be so evident, I do not know; but I do
miss the hares, which I looked upon as my friends. To some

extent these seem to have been replaced by roe deer, which are becoming ever more evident, attractive creatures too. And wild mink, escaped from mink farms, less so perhaps.

On the subject of birdwatchers, if these have greatly proliferated, they are almost always amiable – even when the odd one or two do discover that I am not the Warden, despite my notepad and pencil, and cannot answer all their penetrating questions as to why the tracks are so muddy, and where is the bar-tailed godwit to be found? Nowadays twitchers, as they seem to be called, why I know not, largely carry tripods to steady their telescopes, and dress much more sensibly than of yore. I get on excellently well with the real Wardens, whom I have always found most effective and friendly. I may say that I no longer shoot in the Bay.

The long lines of square concrete tank-traps, relics of 1939—45, have largely gone, having in fact been removed to form bottoming for the great power-station on the coast further west at Cockenzie, thus improving the prospect.

And there is precious little left of the submarines out on the bar; also the abandoned fishing-boats at the Kilspindie side.

My Tess has departed to wherever good, or goodish, dogs go; and, my personal family conditions having changed over the years, she has not been replaced. I miss her. So a lot has altered – but a lot remains the same, I am thankful to say, and despite increasing popularity, the place is nowise spoiled, never giving the impression of being overcrowded, even on a sunny Sunday.

I still set off daily across the footbridge, paper and pen in hand, and still the novels get written; whether the quality improves with long practice or deteriorates with age, is not for me to say – but if the latter, I cannot blame the bridge or the tidelands and dune-country.

Mind you, there was a hiccup in the process recently. In February 1990, in a winter storm, my beloved bridge was

breached and demolished – tragedy! It took until the following November, for one reason or another, for the local
authority to get it rebuilt. Meanwhile many birdwatchers and
others, the more venturesome ones, got wet over the tops of
their wellies, trying to pick their way across the shallows where
the bridge should have been. *I* soon stopped trying to emulate
them, for even if I got across, by the time I came back, the tide
was in and I had to walk miles around to get across the Peffer
Burn. So I had to get my car out every morning, to drive
halfway to Gullane, and then cross the golf course to reach my
desired walking route, since I cannot really write even my
variety of fiction walking along a traffic-busy highway.

However, eventually the new bridge was built, and very fine,
slightly higher than the old one, and very substantial. And the
kindly local authority asked me to open it, I suppose as its most
chronic user, a notable occasion, even if the press photogra-
pher arrived the *next* day.

So there it is, the footbridge, still the access to my enchantment.

NIGEL TRANTER

CHAPTER ONE

Two Paths to Enchantment

I write this crossing the bridge. Its wooden spars drum entic-ingly beneath my sandals. Can wooden spars entice? Assuredly, if they lead in the right direction. Not that these have any need to entice me. I have been lost, their slave, for many a long year. Yet still they quicken my steps, always. Not fast enough yet for Tess, of course; she dances impatiently in the middle of the bridge, fifty yards ahead of me at least, her over-long claws clicking on the wire that binds the spars together. I can never walk fast enough for Tess on the bridge.

I write here and now because this is where I usually start to write. That is the whole point. As the spars creak and drum beneath my feet a sort of ferment starts within me, an eager-ness, an anticipation. Always. It may not always produce words worth writing down, even by my standards; often I score out what I started here. But it starts – that is the importance of it, to me. The urge courses through me and down to my finger-tips. To the ballpoint pen. On to the cut up, folded and stapled-together National Forth Road Bridge Committee plac-ards. We got *that* bridge, in the end, rather sooner than we anticipated, and I inherited a fine store of placards. Enough to write another dozen books on, possibly. WOT, NO BRIDGE? they say. WRITE YOUR M.P. They say NO BRIDGE, NO HOPE, UNLESS YOU AGITATE, YOU DEMAND. SUPPORT

Footbridge to Enchantment

THE COMMITTEE. All that blue ink is rather a nuisance. But on the other side the placards are virgin white – at least, as I set out across the wooden footbridge, they are – and their thin, pliable pasteboard makes excellent material for writing on in the open air, the Scottish East Coast open air. The wind does not tear it, nor does rain soften and pulp it – no, not even the tears from my eyes or the drips from my nose, on occasion. So equipped, I write – and Tess fancy-dances, trembling with eager impatience another thirty yards ahead, glancing wary brown treacle-ball eyes down at the water below, nevertheless.

For it is a long bridge this – though not long perhaps compared with the bridge that the neatly cut up placards urged everyone to fight for. It is exactly two hundred paces long – I know, who pace across it every day. Long for a footbridge, a lowly but elongated footbridge, one yard wide and two hundred yards long, with a dog's-leg bend to counter the action of the tides – just like the Tay Rail Bridge at Dundee. But not so high above the tide, of course. Just five feet high. Indeed, at highest spring tides I have often seen the bridge covered; crossed it that way too, leaping the splashing waves on and on, like a squattering sheldrake that has eaten too much sea zostera-grass and can't get airborne. A lowly footbridge perhaps, with some of its spars in need of repair – but not just any footbridge nevertheless. The Footbridge to Enchantment you might call it, if you happened to be a sentimentalist. My dictionary defines enchantment as the use of magic arts, charm, delight in a high degree.

Tess prefers crossing the bridge when the tide is out. She doesn't like water, even a few feet below her. If ever a man was sold a pup, a genuine dyed-in-the-wool pup, that was myself, five years ago. I suppose that anyone with even a modicum of knowledge about dogs would have known, in the dog-shop, that the sprawling six-week-old bundle of plump tawny satin, velvet ears, and pink tongue too big for its mouth, would *not* turn into a substantial and respectable Golden Labrador which would retrieve shot game, feathered or otherwise, rather than try to outmatch it in its own element, collect my ducks for me when they fell into the water, or even walk decently to heel on occasion. They would have recognised that the inch-long question-mark of a tail would develop longitudinally only, apart from sprouting a notable white tip at its end;

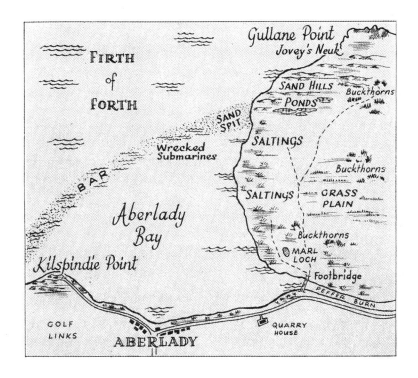

that the plump body would fine down approximately to something on the lines of a whippet, and the blunt little face would mould itself into a fox's leering pointed mask with the large and reproachfully prominent eyes of a baby seal about to be ravished from its mother. I recognised none of this, and

3

paid up. I have been paying up ever since.

Tess generally waits for me at the patch of sand at the far end of the Timber Brig – not out of any dutiful respect for myself, but purely to ascertain which path I will take. This is a matter of supreme unimportance to me, since both tracks are paths to freedom and both reach enchantment in their own good time. I can turn left along the tideline, or go straight before me into the grey-green grass plain of the salt-marsh. Either way there is nothing, and everything, ahead of us – the vast vacant levels of the great bay where the tides ebb and flow over the mud-flats, and the waders bank and swerve and flash in flocks disciplined to a thousandth of a second yet wildly free as the wind; the empty saltings where a million pools and dubs and runnels reflect eternity, and the curlews trill their endless refrain; the far distant bar where, calm or storm, the rollers break in unceasing succession, gleaming white against blue or stark chalk against slate, three miles long of muted thunder; and far far away, half-right, beyond the salt-marsh, beyond distance, unreal and scarcely to be reached, like escarpments of the moon, the dune country, the sand-hill ranges, golden, beckoning, mirage-mountains that seem to hold the sun even on the greyest day, that sing in the wind, where the terns and the eiders and the martins nest and the fox lopes about his affairs. And over all this, and more, dominating it and all the sea beyond, enfolding, reigning supreme and seeming to level even the proud sand-hills into crouching obeisance, the great skies, the soaring cloudscapes, the radiance, the light, the infinite translucent light of the north.

What matters it which path I take – except to Tess?

In winter and spring I tend more often, I suppose, to take the path to the right, inland, as likely to be more dry. There is a gradual slant down to the sea, even in the seemingly level salt-marsh, and since water drains downwards, however sluggishly, the lower track is frequently waterlogged, with the water-table

4

so close to the surface and the tide itself damming up the drainage. Not that I usually make the decision consciously – for what are damp feet when one's head is in the clouds? Though possibly the same shrinking feet are apt to look after themselves and keep themselves dryish more often than I am aware. For certainly Tess, who I think prefers the lower path for obscure reasons not unconnected with the intensely satisfying odoriferous things that not uncommonly are washed up along the tideline – Tess has to swallow her disappointment with notable frequency, and console herself with the frustrating business of trying to catch larks on the wing.

It is extraordinary how quickly the larks take over the moment that one's foot leaves the last plank of the footbridge. I suppose that there must be larks on the unenchanted side of the bridge, also. My house is only three hundred yards away, back there, in a corner of woodland between two fields, and no doubt larks on occasion soar above my garden. But it is a fact that never do I hear them shouting their praise until I cross the bridge – and then immediately, unfailingly, they are all around me, shouting their heads off, rocketing up on all sides, jerkily scaling the heavens like celestial spiders on invisible webs, trilling with an unquenchable exuberance direly calculated to get between any earthbound author and his subject. Strange that the din never seems to penetrate beyond the bridge. It can't all be the fault of the traffic on the North Berwick road. Perhaps it is just that my ears subconsciously and automatically tune in to a different wavelength.

I am much enamoured of those larks. So is Tess – but she has never yet managed to catch one, soar into the air as she will, with agonised twistings of her lissome yellow body, to try to gain the extra inch or two.

I wonder why it is that larks never sing on the ground? It can't only be to avoid giving away the sites of their nests, for I have watched the same lark rise and land time and again in half-a-dozen different positions, throbbing with joyous sound immediately on taking the air but silent as the grave again the moment its feet touch the ground. I can only believe, with the poet, that the creature is indeed not of this earth at all but only blithe spirit to which the mundane terrestial touch must bring appalled silence.

I suppose that there must be literally thousands of larks' nests between the footbridge and the ultimate sand-hills; yet only once have I ever stumbled upon one. This can't be merely because I am unobservant, or too preoccupied with my note-book, for I find great numbers of other nests – belonging to redshanks, meadow-pippits, partridges, eiders, even to the tiny wrens. It may be just that the larks, in doing things to me, also manage to pull wool over my eyes in this matter. In which case, I can only believe that they do the same to the carrion crows, those sardonic black devils that are the only influence that I feel to be really out-of-tune with this enchanted place of mine, the serpents in the garden; for though these litter the ravished egg-shells of every other kind of nest all over the wide grass plain, never do I see larks' eggs amongst this pathetic debris.

I do not deny that this pleases me, quite irrationally.

For, of course, I am not foolish enough to be against predators – like many dear kind ornithologists that I could mention. Or perhaps it is unfair to name them ornithologists, a term which implies the more scientific and objective approach? Birdwatchers will do, nature-lovers, bursting with an all-embracing and militant affection for all birds and beasts that look or seem so pretty, attractive, or interestingly unusual – but turn a blind and chilly eye upon other species less charmingly endowed, such as starlings, rats, mice, bats at rest (in the gloaming air, of course, they are entirely and romantically acceptable) crows and many of their fellow-men.

There I go, on one of my hobby-horses which I must on no account mount. How tiresome are folk with such chips on their shoulders I am only too well aware. Delete, if you please.

I was talking about crows and other predators. The Creator made them that way, undoubtedly for very good reason. They preserve the balance of nature, a thing that mankind is ever ready to upset; they keep the rest of nature on its toes, countering the degeneration of species by weeding out weaklings that would otherwise breed poor stock; they act as very necessary scavengers. But crows, somehow, are different; to me, at any rate. They are such spivs, such cynical and unprincipled killers. I have watched a crow peck a hole in every green egg of seven in an eider-ducks down-lined nest high on a sandhill, and then deliberately tip each one out so that it rolled away down the steep sand slope to smash itself on the stones below. That without any sucking or eating of the contents of one of them, and with the frantic mother duck wheeling and flapping around in heart-rending agitation. Why did I not interfere then, you ask? Because I had already done so, had driven the raider off – only to see it, through my glasses, ten minutes later with me safely out of the way, return to its amusement.

It is the sheer intelligence of crows, their mocking cunning, which, allied to their evil deeds, upsets me. A stoat or a weasel, of which there are plenty across my bridge, I suppose, is just as savage and heartless, and will kill for the sheer joy of killing. But somehow these are not so indecent about the business, more determinedly and naturally fierce; not so blatantly, so calmly and almost casually unrelenting in their evil-doing.

Or am I talking nonsense? My hate, perhaps, is partly sour grapes. For I find the creatures practically impossible to shoot. With a gun, they laugh at me – and to a shooting man, that is anathema. When I have no gun, it is different; they will let me approach within two or three yards of them before flapping off with heavy disdain. I have tried carrying a stick under my arm, of the same length as a shotgun, and even pointing it at them from my shoulder; but they are never deceived, merely waiting until I am almost within striking distance before ruffling disreputable dusty feathers and launching themselves from buckthorn or flotsam with a derisive croak. But let me have the twelve-bore with me, however innocently disguised, and they won't let me within a hundred yards – despite the valid permit to shoot the brutes that I also carry.

Perhaps I should explain. Aberlady Bay is a Local Nature Reserve, within the meaning of the Act – The National Parks and Access to the Countryside Act 1949. By no other token would you know that it was such a thing, I'm happy to say, or anything other than just a notably empty and unusually flat and roadless corner of the coastline, strangely remote to be within sixteen miles of the Capital of Scotland. There is a noticeboard at the disenchanted end of the bridge, admittedly, setting forth seventeen by-laws, with the seventeenth officially cancelled as a highest-level afterthought – and the why and the wherefore of that is a story in itself, into which I had better not launch myself. But that is about as far as the reserve business goes. Here is no artificial sanctuary, no man-made preserve, no enclosure of any sort; just an unspoiled stretch of our island littoral left that way, with access free as the winds that blow across it. As well it might be. I fought long and hard to keep it that way – and, of course, keep my cherished duck shooting as well. The fight was not entirely successful in the latter respect, so that the mallard and widgeon that flight at dusk and dawn now may only be shot on permit in Aberlady Bay – or shot at, shall we say, with more accuracy? My other permit, as a member of the Local Management Committee, to shoot crows in the interests of the conservation of other birds, is indeed probably the only interference with the normal natural sequence that does take place – and precious little it amounts to, as I have confessed.

But why waste time on crows, the only flaw in an otherwise varied and lovely tapestry? Or by-laws either? The trouble is, of

9

course, that the crows, like the by-laws, like laws generally today, proliferate and increase notably year by year. Just where the link is, escapes me for the moment, but obviously there is a distinct if hidden affinity between the genus carrion crow (*Corvus corone corone*) and that of the greater or lesser bureaucrat (*Vultur vulgaris major* or *minor*).

Tess is wiser. She studiously ignores all such. Obviously crows, if not by-laws, embarrass her. Besides, there are much more interesting things close at hand. Only some four hundred yards from the bridge-end are two large jungly clumps of buckthorn, and between them a reedy irregular sheet of water, perhaps a couple of acres in extent, known as the Marl Loch. Presumably this was once a marl or gravel pit. Now it is a haunt of moorhens and snipe, of sedge and willow warblers. In late spring and early summer it is ablaze with yellow flag iris, and redolent of the scent of spearmint. Sheltered by the buckthorns, insects breed here in quantities and varieties suggestive of the tropical swamps, and in consequence, of a warm evening, the swifts and swallows will stage a massed aerial display of such complexity, density and velocity as to defy the human eye, the comprehension, almost the belief. Has anyone ever witnessed or heard of a mid-air collision of these birds, even when they are so closely assembled that the air seems positively to teem with them? When, as must often happen, more than one dives at the same insect? When the disturbance of the air around them, lashed by a thousand wings, must be an aeronautical nightmare? Has anyone ever computed the speed of a swallow's dive, I wonder? How do they do it? Is there some built-in millionth-of-a-second form of radar, some faster-than-lightning intercommunication system, an automatic aero-dynamic compensation for the chaotic effects of air disturbance?

It seems that we have a long way to go, in our vaunted scientific conquest of the air.

The buckthorns that flank this Marl Loch, and are creeping right round it, hold their own interest and problems – apart from providing dense and spiky thickets where a host of creatures, from owls to pheasants, from lolloping hares to scuttling voles, may hide. The balance of nature can swing in many directions, and tip over into the vegetable world. Mankind has been very clever in so thoroughly and gruesomely destroying the ubiquitous rabbit – but did not pause to consider all the results, other than increased farmers' crops. The by-products have been legion, particularly in the ecology of such lonely places as Aberlady Bay, where the rabbits have swarmed from earliest recorded times. Ancient maps, indeed, refer to the entire area as a warren; and Robert Louis Stevenson, in his *Catriona*, describes it thus:

'Few parts of the coast are lonelier . . . such a shining of sun and sea, such a stir of wind in the bent-grass, and such a bustle of down-popping rabbits and up-flying gulls, that the desert seemed to me like a place alive.'

Now, after centuries, the down-popping rabbits are gone, save for the odd furtive survivor. Now, also, there is nothing to keep the buckthorns in check. For the rabbits ate the tender young green shoots projecting above ground from busy prob-ing roots that thrust outwards in all directions – and that a year or two later are transformed into tough jagged bushes which are all but indestructible, and of which Christ's crown of thorns is traditionally supposed to have been plaited. Useful, controlled buckthorn can be, being frequently planted to provide shelter-belts, to anchor shifting sands, and so on; but since, uncontrolled, it spreads in every direction at the rate of between two and three feet a year, it is rapidly changing the appearance of the landscape in many areas. Like many an-other, I had no idea that the rabbits were so effectively holding it in check, until the year after myxomatosis. In the years since, most of the clumps have more than doubled their size and are still spreading at a compound rate. I hate to think what Aberlady Bay will be like twenty years from now, unless the rabbits come back.

Another similar but more pleasant development is the growth of little scattered hawthorn trees, all over the heathlands here. Presumably the rabbits destroyed these seedlings formerly also, for I never noticed such a thing rising above the tussocky bent-grass. Now there are scores of well-doing little trees, which the snell salt sea-winds do not seem to distress. How high they will grow remains to be seen, but already some rise to over ten feet. It may be, in time to come, that the whole character of this grass-plain will change, and its bird and animal life with it. But I fear that in that case it will be the buckthorns that will win the race.

Change, of course, is a continual and universal process, however much we like to close our eyes to it – and however little it may appear in a superficial glance at an area like this, which I myself have frequently and quite inaccurately declared, with a sort of personal pride, to have remained unchanged in ages, in aeons. The sand-dunes are forever altering shape and size; the tide creeps further and further in here, and further out there, exposing or covering rocks and reefs; new dew-ponds and drainage lochans appear, and others dry up; one kind of wildfowl will flock to the Bay, and then disappear as though unknown. But these are all within the normal and accepted scheme of things. Less readily to be accepted is the sort of dire and radical change that, because it strikes at man's own permanence and stature, seems to knock somewhat ominously at some well-closed door within us, where we carefully bottle up irrational and atavistic fears. We all look askance at change, the fear of the unknown, a safety device born in all humanity, as in all the animal kingdom.

Even out here, there is that sort of change, sufficient to give us pause perhaps, to make us wonder. Unlikely as it may seem, this wild and vacant heath was once the haunt of men – and better still, of sprightly young ladies. And by once, I do not mean in some dim and distant past, nor by haunt do I mean a suitably unfrequented corner for discreet love-making or even Sunday afternoon walking. For here, believe it or not, used to be a pleasure ground, a kind of forerunner of the present day lido – although, admittedly, for the bathing belles one would have to go further out towards the sea proper. I have by me a guide-book of Aberlady district, published in no more remote a period than 1926, in which two grass tennis courts here are enthusiastically advertised; now, search as I will amongst the reeds and tussocks, I can find no trace of their site. A curling-pond was here also – though this can still be distinguished from the other pools and lochans by its oblong and regular shape. In 1938, when I first came to Aberlady to live, the ruins of a golf clubhouse, modest but stone-built, still remained, like the curling-pond and presumably the tennis courts, within a hundred or two yards of the Marl Loch and the footbridge. Now, nothing – not even a rickle of stones.

This also is the sort of thing that gets between a novelist and his notebook.

It is not quite so inexplicable as it seems, perhaps. Curiously, it all stems from a sort of feudal rivalry, an echo of the era when lords and lairds ruled us all, rather than the bureaucrats. Under God, of course. The village of Aberlady, almost a mile away on the other side of the bay, has always been a golfing community, and had its own little golf course nearby. Then, in the 1860s, Lord Elcho, who later succeeded as Earl of Wemyss, the local magnate, seems to have been bitten by the military bug and became a great enthusiast for the Volunteer movement. Nothing would do but that tiny and sleepy Aberlady should forthwith became an example and an edification, in this matter, to the rest of Victoria's empire-ruling realm. A drill-hall was built – now the Community Association's hall, gifted by the Earl of Wemyss – and a shooting-range was obligatory. Not desirous of having such a thing within his own extensive policies of Gosford House, his lordship decided that the only place for it was on the stretch of sea links north of the village where Aberlady played its golf – where indeed even King James played golf three hundred years before when he was forced to make some sort of gesture in that respect to account for his frequent visits to the ladies of Gosford. Sadly the golfers had to bow to the militant militarist.

However, there was, and is, another lairdship over at my side of the Bay, almost equally old-established, and which has not always seen eye-to-eye with the noble proprietors aforementioned. Hope of Luffness now allowed the bereft sportsmen to contrive a new golf course just across the wooden footbridge, being a golfer himself. Whether the curling-pond was already there, I do not know – but almost certainly the tennis courts would follow on, for the ladies.

Then, some twenty or thirty years later, the tide turned. The laird had a disagreement with his fellow golfers, and refused to renew the lease. So again Aberlady's sportsmen were homeless – which was sad, for they seem to have been a worthy and patient lot. It is on record that in May 1875 there was a notable match between them and Glasgow Golf Club, no less, sixteen men a side, over this same now vanished course; the Aberlady men won by no fewer than ninety-two holes in the two rounds. They knew the holes, of course. There would be celebrations in the little Golf Hotel in Aberlady's main street, that night.

Lord Elcho, now Earl of Wemyss and presumably disillusioned with soldiering, stepped in again, in reproof of Laird Hope, and back across the Bay the golfers trooped. Kilspindie Golf Club, on the original site but somewhat extended, is the result, now a popular course for many city sportsmen. One of the stone butts of the rifle range still stands in the middle of the course, but the sea has swallowed the other. It is edifying to note that Mr Hope, not to be outdone, founded a new Luffness Golf Club on a course just a little further to the east, which likewise still flourishes today in opposition.

Footbridge to Enchantment

There is a lesson here, somewhere, I feel, if I could only track it down. Perhaps a Prime Minister of Denmark put his finger on it one time, when, being brought down this coast by car, and shown the scenery on the way, he commented later to the Provost of North Berwick:

> 'I am interested to note, sir, that all the land which is totally unfitted for golf courses is here given over to agriculture'

These, however, are not the enchantments which I set out to recount. These are the diversions by the way – any writer's unfailing pitfalls. It is something quite otherwise that draws me out here, day in, day out, fine weather or foul, out past the buckthorn, across the heaths, over the salt-marsh, on and on to the sand-hill country, where the sun always seems to be shining, where the eiders croon and the shags play at being Roman standards, where the porpoises gambol and the seals see-saw on the rocks, where anything may happen, indeed, and a man can lose himself or find himself. That something is the place, whether long rollers smash themselves in spray to fill the tingling air with drifting mist, or gentle wavelets work lace-edged embroidery to an azure sea along mile after mile of golden strand; whether the great strung-out echelons of the wild geese trumpet their exciting challenge into the winter's wind, or the slender terns, the swallows of the sea, squabble the long summer days away by the whispering tideline.

A strange, a vagrant, a shockingly lazy and irresponsible life for a man, you say, this beach-combing? Perhaps. It may be that I am selfish, disorientated, off-beam or off-beat – I do not know. But if so , I am unrepentant anyway. I swear that it is a better, happier, more satisfying place in which to earn one's living than most must put up with.

For that is what I am doing out there, of course – earning my living. As surely as one man goes each morning to the office

16

and another to the factory – though the living itself is a deal less sure, I grant you that! For many years, ever since the war, I have written my novels this way, while walking – on the hoof, as it were. Indeed it was the war that started it; previous to that I had written more or less in the conventional and respectable way. But hurled headlong into the Royal Army Service Corps as a full private at 19/- a week – albeit singled out by the perspicacious personnel selection officers as highly suitable material for a mobile printing unit, with an acting unpaid lance-corporal's stripe – it behoved me, with a wife and two young children and a home to maintain, to continue to produce novels, even in His Majesty's time. I did so; I wrote four and a half novels during my Army service, heaven helping me, and whatever the result. But these, such as they were, were not achieved in any kind of cloistered quiet, or even at an office desk; my printery was much more mobile than that, and consisted largely of turning the handles of duplicating machines on wheels. Off-duty time offered all the amenities of 22-man barrack-huts and crowded NAAFI canteens. So I took to the roads and the by-ways, where, even though it could be wet and cold and dark, at least I could be alone, I could hear myself think. Needless to say, I wrote more in summer under such conditions than in winter. I still do, for that matter.

Even when, after a couple of years, I was commisioned into the Royal Artillery – strangely, and through no choice of my own – I still continued to write this way. Even a junior officer has only a modicum of privacy, and a mess is not so different from a NAAFI, and so it became a fixed habit, and I found that I could scarcely write any other way.

That, then, is my excuse. And one can rationalise some sense into it, I submit. Constant movement, it may well be, stimulates the mind – my mind, anyway. One keeps fit – which is important if one has to turn out an average of 1500 finished words daily throughout the year, and a sluggish liver, for instance, can so strongly urge otherwise. Besides, so much of what I write, wisely or otherwise, is set outdoors, in fresh air and action, that it is surely fair that it should be penned that way?

So there it is. And, given these requirements, could anyone show me a more apt and suitable tract of country in which to

operate? Once across the footbridge I can walk for almost unlimited miles without distractions, without seeing a road, without coming near a house or any work of man – save the bathing belles of Gullane beach. Ten miles and more, I can walk, round that scalloped and lovely coast, before I need turn back because of the houses of North Berwick. Not that I often get as far as that.

Without distractions, did I say?

CHAPTER TWO

Boundless Dune Country

The sand-hills lie the best part of two miles from the road –
which of course has been the saving of the place; while anyone
may leave car or bus and cross over the enticing footbridge,
surprisingly few will face those two miles – and another two
back, of course – in these days of moribund leg muscles.
Especially as the long level grass plain in between, to the
uninitiated, may look dull and boring – not to mention wet on
the feet. So be it. I know of many Aberlady residents who have
lived all their lives here, and have never so much as set foot on
the planks of the bridge, much less headed out towards those
distant glowing ranges. Indeed, it is probable that not one in
ten of the villagers has ever been there – and the same applies
to Gullane, the slightly larger community a couple of miles or
so to the east; only more so. In over forty years, I believe that
I could count almost on the fingers of my two hands all the
local people whom I have seen out there.

I am not weeping over it, mind you – only wondering.

The dune country is an extraordinary place in every sense
of the word. Not large in prosaic acres and miles, as it were on
the map, but curiously extensive, measureless, far-flung, when
you get there, not amenable to footrule assessments. I suppose
that the true overall acreage of the sand-hill area, between
Aberlady and Gullane Bays, is less that 500 acres. Yet therein
is a world of its own, a tract to which normal conditions and
reckonings just do not apply – and in which I have come across

strangers quite lost; and not only in the sense of being puzzled, mazed, but physically wandered. And without a single tree, much less a wood, to hem them in.

Moreover, the place is not static. It is ever growing, and changing shape and character – some seasons by very little, some most notably, depending upon imponderable and complex circumstances of wind and weather, time and tide.

Most suitably this fascinating area has no true and accepted name. Modern maps are apt to spread the appellation 'Gullane Links' all over it, but this is quite inapplicable; the links refer to the slightly higher ground of Gullane Hill and Gala Law inland a little, the dune country being neither links nor part of the old Gullane Common which Gullane Golf Course now covers. Older maps use the general term of rabbit warren, though some say 'Yellow Mires' – but the latter obviously relates to the low and wet salt-marsh area before the sand-hills are reached. Local people usually allude to the whole tract as Jovey's or Jova's Neuk, after a semi-legendary figure named Jehovah Gray who lived alone out here at one time, and of whom more anon; but this of course is equally inadequate, for the term neuk or nook belongs only to one little sandy bay or cove amongst many, sandwiched between two out-thrusting spines of rock.

Again, I make no complaint; long may my strange terraqueous domain remain as anonymous as it is boundless and generally fey.

Not that it is to be wondered at that it has no solid or established title, for the place just was not there when the names were being given out. Indeed the old maps show a quite different outline to the coast here, imaginative as early cartographers tended to be in such matters. The fact is that most of this curious area has come out of the sea in comparatively recent times – and, who knows, may equally well go back to it, just as quickly and entirely.

Boundless Dune Country

To comprehend the nature of this entrancing territory, it is probably necessary to understand just a little of the local geography. Aberlady Bay is a vast triangular indentation of the Firth of Forth estuary, drying out at low-water, with a mouth more than two miles wide. Stretching right across this mouth, from east to west and fully another couple of miles out from the head of the Bay, is a huge and wide sand-bar, slightly higher than the floor of the Bay itself, and therefore the first part of the whole to emerge as the tide ebbs. This bar – which is no puny bank, but a semi-submarine tract in itself, half-a-mile wide by four times that length, and the thunder of which, pleasantly faint or sheerly menacing, provides the background music for the entire area even as far inland as my own house – this bar is constantly and unfailingly supplied with replenishments of fine golden sand from somewhere in the bed of the Firth. I say replenishments, for constantly the sand, drying out in the sun, is whipped up and carried away north-eastwards by the prevailing south-westerly winds, to be deposited inevitably along this side of the long ridge of rock which forms the basis of Gullane Hill and ends in the snout of Gullane Point. This continuous process, most pronounced in dry windy weather, results in a curious ridge and valley formation, running east and west, ever-changing, ever extending, with some of the summits reaching approximately seventy-five feet in height. Whether our globe is canting slightly as some suggest, or whether it is merely this corner of Scotland that is quietly adjusting itself, every year sees the sea cutting deeper into Jovey's Neuk itself, to the east, and at the same time swinging away outwards at the western end, where the bar begins, allowing room for new sand ranges. These, in a surprisingly short time, are covered over with the spiky grey-green marram grass, and later, with tussocky bents, and so merge imperceptibly into the landscape. To the uninitiated it is often almost unbelievable that a substantial range of hillocks, perhaps

21

quarter-of-a-mile long and a score of feet in height, rippling green in the breeze, was just not there three years ago.

This surprising and topsy-turvy terrain seems to have its own curious effect on more than myself and the folk who occasionally get lost amongst the identical sand-hills and ridges. Fauna and flora establishing themselves here are likewise affected. I have played hide-and-seek with foxes amongst the dunes. Just what the fox finds to attract him out here I do not know – but many a morning, on the night-smoothed sand, I see his neatly-aligned, determined-looking tracks, so much more single-minded, somehow, than any dog's.

Once I met three whooper swans, marching along in single file round the foot of a large dune, all in step and apparently on serious business bent. They showed none of the alarm and suspicion with which such creatures usually eye approaching man; indeed they ignored me entirely, though only a few yards away, stalking on past without so much as a glance, their feet pacing out a steady left-right, left-right. Somehow, I felt exceedingly foolish.

Then there is the green woodpecker which haunts Gullane Point and these sand ranges. Do not ask me what it lives on, or why it should come back here season after season – for a less suitable habitat for a woodpecker would be hard to conceive, with not a tree in sight. Yet it struts about amongst the bents, suns itself on the rocks, or swoops around in its peculiar low-level looping flight, as though here alone it found what life held for it. A misogynist perhaps – for I have never seen more than this dedicated single bird.

The plant world can behave as oddly here. I said that there were no trees – which is true – but sycamores do grow, though not as trees. They flourish as little thickets, behaving rather as does the buckthorn, though not ferociously, spreading farther out each year with new little shoots rising straight out of the ground but never attaining more than a couple of feet in height and the thickness of a pencil. Presumably it is all something to do with the roots feeling outwards and upwards for their moisture, not downwards into the dry sand, a moisture insufficient to support more than these slender stalks. Yet none of these curious sycamore thickets grow in the spreading marshlands and heath nearby, where there is moisture in plenty. And the humble and despised hogweed, that dull excrescence the common or garden cow-parsnip, here reverses the process, growing positively gigantic like the Biblical mustard-seed, so that I have seen the fowls of the air, if not actually lodging in the branches thereof, at least roosting there, and have sometimes myself taken shelter beneath them in a shower of rain – where shelter is hard to come by.

Stranger blooms than this decorate the sand-hills on occasion, curious exotic plants that I have known to grow nowhere else, the seeds of which I can only imagine to have been brought in by the tides from goodness knows what far and unlikely places. I am insufficient a botanist to name them, and they seldom last long enough for me to bring more knowledgeable identification to bear, springing up in the sun-hot sand, flowering briefly and vividly, and dying in a day or two. I remember a rich red orchid-like flower blooming alone on the bare sand like a scrap of maroon velvet, and drawing me by its glow from quite a distance – but gone the next day so that I could not even trace where it had been.

Of more permanent growth is the great horned poppy which proliferates amongst the dunes, never failing to surprise me with the sight of its luscious waxy lemon-yellow blooms, more like a prinked up-tulip than any poppy, so out of keeping somehow with its barren surroundings. I have seen it nowhere else.

The sweet briar is another prevailing asset, and its scent delicately perfumes the salt-laden air whenever one moves

23

down-wind of one of the many clumps.

That scent, like others, can have a curious and unlooked-for effect. On me, at any rate. I suppose that scents are even more evocative than sights and sounds, and frequently, when I pass one of these sweet briars, I am transported immediately and comprehensively back into some specific scene of an earlier novel on which presumably I had been working when under the influence of this individual perfume. It can be quite upsetting, if the current story is going well at the moment, for once the sequence and tempo is more than superficially disturbed, it may take some time to get fully back into the mood; especially if, as is probable, the basic mood and aura of the earlier tale is radically different from the present one – for it is the briar's story that is all of a sudden much the stronger. Another aspect of it, equally strange, is the fact that there are many briar bushes, and the transposition does not work every time; nor does each bush produce the same scene of the same novel. I suppose that I have written well over seventy novels out on this terrain, so that it is perhaps not to be wondered at if the emanations become a little tangled sometimes. But what I want to know is – do the different bushes, which all seem to smell alike to me, in fact each have their own slightly distinctive scent, to account for this varied impact, recognised, but not consciously, by my not very acute nose? Or is it the location which some ridiculous part of my mind, which should be concentrating on the job in hand, links with the scent to produce the appropriate flashback?

How galling to sense hidden depths in oneself, and utterly fail to plumb them.

I must not forget the teasels amongst my curious crops. They grow here too, a most unusual plant in this part of Scotland, prickly mops on long stalks, that rustle dryly in the breeze. Again I know of no other haunt of the teasel – apart from those it shares with the aspidistra in front parlours left

Boundless Dune Country

over from the Victorian era.

Does anything strike you about all this indigenous and very individual flora? If you walked with me hereabouts, it very quickly would – and, if you were not careful, in rather painful fashion. I refer to the prickliness of practically everything, the spiky jagged quality of almost all that grows and flourishes in this sandy paradise. For each blade of the marram grass is armed with a tip sharp as a needle, and the entire area is thick with every kind of thistle in the book. The buckthorns and the sweet briar, the hawthorns and the teasels, the wild gooseberries and the yellow gorse – all one approaches with caution and touches at one's peril. Pitfalls for the unwary writer with his head in his own vapourish clouds.

The deserts sprout their camel-thorn and prickly-pear and cactus, of course. Is it the sand that does it? Is it some natural safety device, where plant-life is sparse and its roots vital to bind and hold down the shifting dunes? To ward off the plant-eaters, who, in destroying these, would destroy all?

It is a pretty theory, anyway.

Not that there are many herbivores at Jovey's Neuk, now that the rabbits have gone, to endanger the flora. Though once the residents of Gullane had common rights here, and could and did graze their cattle over the bents and heaths. It would be interesting indeed if some of them started to do so again, for though the County, now District, Council, coolly assuming itself to be their representative and official agent, handed over the higher parts to the golf course, now famous – that does not necessarily mean that the common rights, vested from time immemorial in the heritors of the village, have been wiped out. Being something of an upholder of public rights – also, I fear, something of an anarchist by nature – few gestures would please me more than to see this little matter being contested by those who may have the right to do so.

25

Be that as it may, today the hares more or less have the area to themselves – and whatever they eat, it is obviously not the young shoots of buckthorn and the like. A pity that it is not, for the hares are legion, strange other-worldly creatures that I feel are never quite all there, not only in March – and I do not mean that in any derogatory way. It is amazing how they have multiplied, out here, since the rabbits departed. This has been reported, I understand, from other areas, but nowhere that I have heard of has the increase been so marked as here. The reason for it, like so much else, escapes me. Was it that the rabbits ate all the food, previously? Surely not. Or just that the hares did not like their cousins, and would not come where the latter swarmed?

Whatever the cause, the change is for the better, I assert, as far as the sand-hill country is concerned. The dreamy lolloping hares are far more suitable denisons of this strange out-of-this-world territory than all Stevenson's down-popping scurrying rabbits. They are curious abstracted, preoccupied creatures, that once in my ignorance I thought to be characterless, brainless, plain stupid. Daft they may be, but now I know them better and respect their daftness.

I was not alone in my error; hares are very commonly misjudged. They are, I think, the poets of the animal world, concerned with other values than the material – and we all know how often poets are considered to be a little mad. Much more so than novelists. Hares do not live to eat, as so much of creation does, most obviously; indeed in the times without number that I have watched them, in remarkably few have they been actually feeding. Playing, alone or with others, contemplating infinity, washing by wetting and using their forepaws, chasing butterflies – yes, I once watched a hare doing that – or merely out on a quiet hopping stroll, they seem to have minds above their bellies. Perhaps they eat early in the morning when I am not about to see – but if so that by no means alters the issue. They use the long daylight hours for other ends, and while I would hesitate to declare their entire philosophy of life, a great deal of their time is clearly taken up with a sort of ambulant pensiveness – appreciated perhaps by an ambulant writer – and indulging a gentle sense of fun.

It is this latter propensity that has given them the reputation for madness – a sad reflection on mankind, when you come to think of it. Admittedly they may indulge in some rather crazy antics at the mating season; but then, do not some of even the most dignified of us? I have known a clergyman of middle years, in pursuit of his love . . . ah, well – perhaps we need not go into that. The mating urge only heightens and makes plain to the least observant this sense of fun, which I believe to be an important part of the hare's make up at all times. Out in the sand-hills I see them at all seasons of the year. I have watched them, all unawares, run zig-zagging from side to side of a track, back and forward, as a child will do on the way home from school; leap abruptly high in the air, and somehow come down looking the other way, all but laughing; play hide-and-seek with other hares amongst the clumps and tussocks; pretend to run away from Tess and myself in alarm, only to reappear moments later behind us, peering sideways round a dune.

Possibly even the Creator's act in putting hares' eyes away round at the side of their heads so that in fact they look outwards, not forwards, has added to their reputation for foolishness, for if they are much interested or concerned with what may be going on at one side or the other, they may well lope smack into your legs without noticing you – which to many is proof positive of the sheerest folly. Yet, is there not another way of looking at it? Presumably the All Wise did not make this creature to look outwards instead of forwards like most of His creation, out of a mere caprice. If some of the rest of us were so endowed, the world might be a happier place – for it is a rather significant attribute, is it not? I suggest that is

27

why the hare is the least materialistic of animals. Astuteness, it seems to me, is a vastly over-rated quality. Moreover no-one who has watched a hare at close quarters will assert, I think, that those large and liquid brown eyes, so pensive, so reflective, do not look almost as much inwards as outwards. Or am I just blethering again?

Tess loves hares. She is not supposed to chase things, and I used to call her sternly in when she picked up a hot scent and went yelping off after one. Now, I let her go, on most occasions, though not in the breeding season – secure in the knowledge that she will not only do no harm but that she will give the hare more fun even than she gives herself. Prolonged observation has convinced me that the hares enjoy leading a vocally ecstatic Tess around the landscape quite as much as she revels in the process. They halt to allow her almost to catch up when she shows signs of flagging; they slow down to an amble when the lead becomes excessive – as it fairly quickly does, fleet of foot as Tess may be; they swing round in wide circles and back to me and the start of the exercise; they even deliberately turn aside to slip through buckthorn clumps, and turn to watch at the other side how Tess gets on amongst the spikey jags. These cantrips all end the same way, with Tess, panting and exhausted and with her tongue hanging out, unable to utter so much as a squeak – for she always commences squealing her excitement at the pitch of her lungs, thus handicapping herself sorely – and the hare sitting up on its powerful hind-quarters, ears cocked, nose twitching, ready to start the whole thing again, cool as a cucumber even after a mile's chase. Obviously one of these extended romps quite makes any hare's day.

Actually it was Tess who really introduced me to hares. I mean formally, as it were. Two or three years ago she found a tiny leveret alone in the snow, and born out of due season, and by her whimpers and gesticulations persuaded my daughter, who had taken her a walk, to come and examine her intriguing discovery – for Tess, though she delights to chase hares and skylark for larks, would never dream of hurting either in the quite improbable event of ever getting near enough to do so; indeed she would be most horribly embarrassed, for she has a notable gift for embarrassment. My daughter was shown a tiny scrap of brown fur, no bigger than her fist, all appealing eyes and up-pricked ears, and which, far from being afraid of her or the dog, adopted them both immediately and started to follow where they went. Tess was greatly disconcerted. Frances May first endeavoured to find the form from which the morsel must have strayed, and then to look for the mother. For once however, there were no hares to be seen in all that landscape – nor tracks thereof. This atomy seemed to have dropped there in the snow from aloft.

The right thing to do was problematical – for though the mother was nowhere to be seen, a pair of busy hunting short-eared owls haunt that area and would not long miss this mite. Other predators would not be far behind. Moreover the creature was quite assured in its own small mind as to what was what, and would not be shaken off. In the end, Frances May decided to interfere with the balance of nature, picked up the small determined character, and brought it home inside her sheepskin jacket, in the belief that otherwise it could not survive.

From that moment, Quarry House revolved round this diminutive entity. You must not suppose that this was on our initiative. We are fond of animals in our household but by no means crazy or maudlin about them, and we all felt that the right place for even a small hare was the great outdoors. But the small hare did not think along those lines at all. It approved of our somewhat rambling establishment, and presumably of ourselves likewise, and proceeded to take charge of both. Never let anyone try to tell you that hares are scatterbrained or irresolute, however abstracted. Mild they may appear to be, but they have wills of steel and a quiet determination that does not know the meaning of defeat – not if Scrap was anything to go by. We became as clay in her tiny but effective hands. She was not to be left alone, and doors must be kept open for her. While preferring the kitchen and its varied activities during the day, she insisted on occupying the exact centre of the sittingroom hearthrug during the evening, where she would sit, like a small ball of brown wool that had developed two ears, seeming to look at the fire but in reality considering my wife and myself in our respective chairs on either side. She washed herself with great thoroughness, sitting up on her hind quarters to do so and using her fore-paws, being particularly concerned about her ears, and frequently holding one right down, the whole inch of it, so that she could lick its black tip properly. She liked to clamber up on to one's knees, needless to say preferring the ladies' laps, and when she felt like a nap, climbing still higher on to their bosoms, to settle there, head and fore-paws up on their necks.

She snored slightly.

Tess she treated as a playmate, of inferior rank and intelligence, from the start – a sort of ignoramus, good for a romp and a tease, but pathetically inexperienced, even of the elementary functions of her own body. She used to try to suck Tess's symbolical teats with much hopefulness, to the latter's grave and anxious offence. She boxed Tess's nose when she could reach up to it, and played with that shameful white tip to her tail, and otherwise misused her. Our cat, Min, a haughty aristocrat of the lowliest origins, she more or less drove out of the house – for an over-developed sense of fun in the very young can be most distressing to dignity and entrenched privilege. Min reached the stage of scarcely appearing indoors below the level of table-top or shelf.

Quarry House throbbed with soulful reproach, determined

frolic, and the curiously loud and impressive thud-thuds of inch-long back feet.

Feeding was a problem, of course, and whether the solution that we adopted – diluted cow's milk fed through an old-fashioned fountain-pen-filler – was the correct one, we never really knew. Not that Scrap was choosy or difficult – quite the reverse; but we felt that certain foods could scarcely be suitable for a week-old hare.

Scrap's life, though brief, was a full one. She became quite a famous hare, in fact, getting into the newspapers and her photograph appearing beside those of film actors and Lord Provosts. My daughter, who remained Scrap's favourite, was then still unmarried, and working as a secretary with a well-known cultural organisation. Twice she took the little creature in to her office in Edinburgh, in her handbag, and Scrap made there such an impact on the august environs of Georgian Charlotte Square as to bring the Press hotfoot on the scene, flashbulbs popping. She took it all in her competent small stride, finding amusement in all things and offence in none. Nor fear. She would drop off to sleep at the slightest provocation, even in the middle of a romp, and wake up again, refreshed and ready for more, two minutes later.

That was when I began to perceive that there was more to hares than I had suspected. Nevertheless, we started mildly to wonder what we would do with a large and full-grown hare lolloping about the premises, demanding to come to town with us, and so on.

We need not have concerned ourselves. She slept in a little wooden box that my son Philip made for her, in a nest of hay, in the kitchen near Tess's bed, for company. Exactly ten days after she had adopted us, ten busy, active days with never a moment squandered, we found her in the morning, hunched up in her usual attitude of sleep – but dead. Of what she died there was no indication. Probably just wrong feeding –

31

although there was no sign of undernourishment, and she had eaten as well as usual, and been as frisky as ever, the night before. No warning, no previous weakening and no vestiges of sickness left behind. Scrap just passed on, on her determined journey.

My wife buried her, wrapped in a silk handkerchief, underneath a clump of violets in a corner of the garden beneath the trees. She wept a little – but personally I am quite satisfied that Scrap's lively, questing fun-full spirit just went thud-thudding off across the road, over the Timber Bridge and the salt-marsh, back to the sand-hill country, where it romps still amongst the dunes, probably chasing butterflies.

CHAPTER THREE

Flotsam and Jetsam

Scrap was not the only foundling with which I got involved over that footbridge. Or not exactly over but *on* the bridge. One morning, I perceived that Tess had halted halfway across – a thing that she normally never does, in case I should change my mind and turn back from the gates of freedom – and was sniffing at something on the planking of the bridge itself. On investigation I was even more surprised than Tess. It was a

kitten, a tiny fluffy smoke-grey ball of the sort known as 'half-Persian', little if any larger than had been Scrap, spitting, however, fiercely in Tess's face, clinging on to one of the wooden splats with all the claws of one small forepaw, the other raised to cuff the dog's enquiring nose, while the woolly little hind-legs alternately scrabbled at the underside of the planking or bicycled in space. How this defiantly miniature object arrived there will ever remain a mystery. Apart from my own establishment and one other cottage a few hundred yards on, there is no house near enough to have produced such a short-legged creature. Its fur was not wet at all – which disposed of the unpleasant notion that somebody might have thrown it into the water from the bridge to dispose of it by drowning, and that it had somehow managed to climb out again. I have never seen any other cats about here, tame or semi-wild. It was just one of those things.

This wide-blue-eyed innocent I picked up, suffering lacerations in the process, and carried along to the aforementioned cottage, assuming that it must have come from there. The lady of the house however disclaimed all knowledge – while ex-claiming at the attractiveness of this unusual piece of flotsam or jetsam. But her children, once they had set eyes on the entity, clamorously adopted it forthwith – and wherever it had come from, it had found its destination.

The kitten remained an integral part of this family thereaf-ter. Sometimes we saw her prowling around our own house and sometimes glimpsed her in the various woodlands nearby; but never again did I see her near the bridge or the tide's edge. Moses, I don't suppose, ever returned to his bulrushes.

I mentioned flotsam and jetsam back there. This is perhaps one of the prime attractions of my enchanted territory for others – not that I can claim to be immune by any means, as you will see, from the fascinations of beach-combing. I do not understand what set of circumstances is responsible, what special conjunction of currents, what configuration of the coastline – but surely never was there such an unfailing repository for bric-a-brac, *objets d'art* and miscellaneous oddi-ties, as that stretch of the eastern shore of Aberlady Bay for half-a-mile on either side of the sand spit at the root of the bar. I have heard it suggested that coastal municipal rubbish-dumps at Edinburgh and Musselburgh are partly responsible – or, alternatively, at Kirkcaldy across the estuary in Fife; but since a great deal of the treasure trove is clearly of foreign origin, this by no means wholly answers the question. I sup-pose that ships coming in to the Firth of Forth ports further up-river might jettison a certain amount of gear – or have it washed overboard – but surely in nothing like the quantities apt to be involved here. I wish that I could remember all the peculiar items that I have stumbled upon. A pair of Dutch sabots, for instance, a little worn, found washed up only a couple of hundred yards apart – to become miniature window-boxes at my home. A first-aid box, with the Danish flag painted on it. A black-and-white painted notice saying NO SMOKING in French. A pair of bellows, with Spanish leatherwork, some-what nibbled. And so on.

Such exotic items are only the *bizarrerie* of the tideline, of course. The general stock-in-trade is sufficiently varied and intriguing – and unexpected. Who, for instance, would expect to find hundreds of yards of excellent quality and apparently new fire-hose coiled like a deflated sea-serpent along the beach? Or a handsome perambulator, intact save for the tyre of one wheel? Or yet some hundreds of 2lb watertight tins of hard-tack biscuits – edible, although enjoyed by Tess more than myself? Wooden objects, of course, preponderate – and they are legion. Apart from the general run of planks and boxes, batons and beams, are to be found chair legs, chair seats, indeed entire chairs, both of the hand and arm variety; many a winter's night I have sat, enthroned in sodden rexine, waiting for the ducks to flight. Bookcases and bedsteads, brushes and breadboards, washboards and walking sticks. Lavatory-seats are a speciality – I have counted as many as eleven of these, of differing quality but basic similarity, on one mile of shore. Pondering the wherefore can be distracting for a writer.

Then there is the rubber-goods and plastics division. Hot-water-bottles, rubber tyres and inner tubes, of course, come in daily. Children's toys, such as rubber dolls, plastic boats, water-pistols and the like, are usually present in large numbers – not to mention beach-balls, sea-borne from sandy bays near and far. Great sheets and lumps and knobbles of crude rubber, hard and heavy, come in from time to time, some almost heavier than I can lift – whence I know not, unless some wartime ship-load sank somewhere and the cargo is gradually coming ashore. Plastic sheeting too, is a fairly frequent offer-ing, some of excellent quality – and certain of my son's friends and climbing colleagues now camp with such material both above and below them on Highland hills. A real problem is presented by the new plastic squeezable containers for detergents, which are practically indestructible and unsinkable. They are floating in by the thousand all round our coasts, and a new occupation layer is building up at high-water mark for future archaeologists to date the neo-plastic period of man's history, the flowering of the squeezee age.

Baskets are a favourite crop – I can seldom bring myself to leave a good basket lying, especially the handsome and commodious herring-crans – washed off trawlers presumably – that make such excellent log-baskets for the fireside. Though these tend to get filled up with the said suitable logs and tempting firewood billets on the way home, attaining great weight and entailing much exhaustion and muscle-ache *en route* – when no writing gets done, needless to say.

Altogether the tide-line is a distinct menace to me, however much Tess approves of it and its fascinating smells. Moreover my family, beneficiaries in a big way though they are, howl ungratefully now at almost every windfall that I deliver. When my wife announces the need for some new household plenishing, great or small, the inevitable outcry arises that, give him time and Father will bring it back with him from Jovey's Neuk. An exaggeration, I feel.

As I have indicated, however, I am by no means alone in this preoccupation with something-for-nothing – for that matter, whenever my family is inveigled out to the relevant stretch of shore, they immediately become as inveterate pickers up of trifles as I am myself, my wife especially leaving behind her a trail of merely displaced articles which one by one she has discarded in favour of a later temptation. Indeed, when occasionally we take visiting friends of the more energetic variety out walking in this direction, they can be guaranteed almost without exception, however proper and dignified at the outset, to return to civilisation positively laden down with heterogeneous junk, most of it quite useless in my expert opinion, from which they will on no account be parted. I have seen . . . well, never mind!

Of course, theoretically, I am told that all this is highly reprehensible, a thoroughly illegal activity. All such flotsam and jetsam, it is rumoured, is the property of the Crown, via the august office of the Receiver of Wreck. Which is a fascinating thought in itself! Suppose . . .?

A local acquaintance of mine, returning with a fine beam of driftwood on his shoulder was once halted between the foot-bridge and the village by a motor-cyclist who turned out to be a coastguard in disguise. He was sternly warned that he was committing an offence, and ordered to put down the shameful piece of wood forthwith – at the nearest tide's edge. There the beam lay for two or three days – until my friend came along one quiet evening and collected it again. The majesty of the law remained intact, supreme.

A less happy feature of the tideline, here as elsewhere, is the large number of seabirds, particularly guillemots, washed up, their wings and feathers so coated with black fuel-oil waste as to prevent them from flying or diving. This has been a problem for bird-lovers for a long time, of course – but despite regulations about the dumping of the oil from shipping, the situation does not seem to improve. It may well be one of those problems which in fact defy solution – for ships must get rid of the waste, and the oil floats on the surface of the sea, in thick black scum or in myriad globules, and is bound to drift in with the tides.

What to do with the victims? I am afraid that nowadays I usually just wring their necks, to put the poor creatures out of their misery. In most cases, undoubtedly, they have been so exhausted and starved before allowing themselves to drift ashore that they are beyond any successful amateur nursing. The oil is exceedingly difficult to wash off, moreover, whatever solution is used – and the fowl seldom make co-operative patients. Also the diet question is a major one, for these divers like their fish live, and in my experience much prefer to starve to death than to have any truck with food defiled by humans. It is a sad situation.

It is strange, to me, that I never find any eider duck oiled up in this way, considering the large numbers of eiders that haunt Gullane Point, and the other headlands in the vicinity, these days. The numbers have increased every year since I first came to live here. Now there are many hundreds, swimming in great rafts, just offshore, or preening themselves on the rocks. Somehow they seem to be able to avoid the oil.

The eider is not a beauty amongst ducks. Despite their quite handsome winter plumage of black, white and palest green, the drakes are distinctly clumsy, with their thick heavy bodies and over-large black beaks; and the female is dowdy in the extreme. And yet, one of the prettiest sights to be seen around this coast in early summer can be the eider families, with strings and flotillas of tiny black fluffy ducklings bobbing about in disciplined formations behind their dusky mothers, unconcerned by waves scores of times their own height, full of grace, fun and high spirits. Such occasions, enhanced by the peaceful, soothing crooning call which the eiders sing to the summer seas, are sheer delight, and make me their firm friend.

The ducks and ducklings, that is. The drakes, of course, take no hand in such frolics. They lie well away, out to sea in stodgy colonies of their own. I don't know whether they ever indulge in crooning like their humble ladies, but if so, by the look of them I should imagine that it would sound more like a sulky croak. They don't help to protect their eggs or babies from crows and predators; they don't pluck their chests to line the nests with their famed and lovely down. In fact I can find nothing to say in their favour – except that they are, I suppose, like the rest of us, only as the Creator made them.

Usually the duckling families – up to a dozen in each – stick close together and near their mothers. But one day I came across a small individualist. Right out at the Point there is a freshwater spring – from which no doubt the semi-legendary Jovey Gray drew his supply – led through an old iron pipe set in concrete. The water trickling down into the coarse sand and shell grit below inevitably formed a tiny pool or basin in the shingle, perhaps eighteen inches across, before draining away down to the sea a score of yards off. In this midget pond, as I came for a drink, I discovered one microscopic fowl, three inches of sooty fluff, swimming around in lone but evident

bliss – with not another duck, infant or adult, in sight, save for
the usual rafts that lay like dark lines scored well out to sea. The
creature circled in one direction for a number of turns, then
reversed and went the other way. Each time that it came under
the trickle from the pipe it shook itself, almost jerking itself out
of the water to do so – but making no attempt to avoid the
trickle. For how long it had been thus happily engaged I have
no idea – nor for how long it might have continued, had it not
suddenly looked up and spotted me standing on the mound
just above. Then there was panic indeed. With a scrambling
bound, the ball of down was out of its basin and off down the
shingle beach, tiny legs racing, incipient wings flapping, tum-
bling constantly on its outstretched nose, heading for the sea
and safety. I watched it until the minute speck was lost to sight
amongst the quite large combers, apparently making for Fife.

The increase in eiders at the Point has been paralleled by
that of the seals. Years ago, when first I began to haunt this
coastline, the sight of a seal was a great rarity, something to be
hailed as an event. Now they are to be seen almost any day, by
the sharp-eyed. This applies not only locally, of course, but to
the entire seaboard of south-east Scotland. There seems to be
no doubt that the grey seals are spreading fast and far from the
Farne Islands of the Northumbrian coast where there has
been a colony for a very long time. In the past, the numbers of
Farne seals were kept down by periodic lethal raids of local
fishermen, especially at the breeding season. The seals, of
course, live on fish, being particularly fond of salmon, and are
great robbers of the nets. So that it was war to the knife – or the
cudgel, unfortunately – between them and the fishers of Holy
Island, Seahouses, Berwick and Eyemouth. Then the nature-
lovers made their voices heard, and the Government stepped
in. The seals were protected. Theoretically not before time –
for the slaughter of the creatures, especially the pups, was a
horrible business, mainly brutal clubbing to death on the

rocks. The fishermen objected, but were over-ruled. Now there are said to be between 5,000 and 7,000 seals breeding on the Farnes, and their overflow has spread up the coast for a hundred miles and more, with the Tay estuary now involved, as well as the Forth. On a fishing seaboard, especially a salmon fishing one, this is serious. Conservation of species is always a tricky matter, and the balance of nature – and man's interests – are easily upset.

I became particularly interested in this problem, not through watching the increasing numbers of seals at Jovey's Neuk – which I quite enjoy – but through the necessary research for my novel *Kettle Of Fish,* which deals with the drama of the sea-fishermen's battle with the vested interests in the salmon monopoly of the Tweed – the rights and wrongs and developments of which need not concern us here. But I discovered then that the fishermen contend – and they ought to know, if anybody does – that the seals account for considerably larger numbers of salmon than do the drift-nets, and that the Government, in its regard for the interests of the commercial river-mouth fisheries and the riparian owners of fishing rights up-river, should more properly turn their minds to this major threat to salmon stocks. When experts tell you that a single seal will eat sixteen to eighteen pounds of fish per day, preferably salmon, and there are, say, 6,000 of them to be fed at the mouth of the salmon-famous Tweed alone – then something of the size of the problem becomes apparent. Moreover, when it is realised that seals do not kill and devour salmon as, for instance, wolves do deer, but are apt merely to snap a great single bite out of the live fish's shoulder *en passant,* leaving the rest to be scavenged by lesser predators, then some idea of the cost of this piece of one-sided conservation will be appreciated. The stake and drift-net fishermen take it as a matter of course to find a greater or lesser proportion of these savaged salmon dead in their nets – the seals are cute enough to

recognise the convenience of robbing nets as against cruising
for single fish in the open sea. Add to this the damage that a
single seal, weighing many hundredweights, can do when
entangled in an expensive nylon net that may have cost £50
and more, and something of the fishermen's case may be
understood.

I am not against seals; they are an added attraction to our
coasts. But their numbers must be controlled if essential
interests of men are not to suffer pointlessly. Constant weighing is necessary when authorities, however well-meaning, start
aiding the balance of nature.

What brings the seals into the Firth of Forth estuary? I don't say
that it must be salmon – although the wooden stakes of fixed
nets still project from the hard sands near the Point, showing
that salmon, formerly at least, were here in quantities worthy
of permanent working. Seals eat other fish, of course, though
salmon and sea-trout are their favourites.

I seldom see the seals ashore or on the rocks at Jovey's Neuk
– although no doubt at night they are there. Yet only a few
miles along the coast, at Fidra below Dirleton, they may very
frequently be seen, playing hide-and-seek amongst the skerries,

basking on the rocks, sometimes even see-sawing on a pinna-cle in high good humour. In my own corner they seem to content themselves, in daylight hours at least, with gazing inquisitively at the shore with great round eyes, from about a hundred yards out, cruising amongst the eiders – who ignore them entirely – and occasionally coming in close enough to hoist round head and bottle shoulders out of the shallows, whiskers bristling, like Bairnsfather's Ole Bill prospecting a better 'ole. They have come quite near to me when I have been swimming – within twenty yards or so – to the alarm of Tess, who prefers to remain, as a former Lord Provost of Edinburgh has colourfully put it, 'with feet firmly anchored on terra cotta'.

Dead seals, usually young ones, are quite frequently washed up on the beach – and pathetic pictures they make, flippers wide in puppy-like appeal. Even dead, Tess sniffs at them very warily; perhaps she senses the deadly teeth and vice-like jaws behind the innocent and seemingly chinless features.

CHAPTER FOUR

Puzzles of the Tide's Edge

Not only Tess and myself, with the occasional beachcombers, find the tideline a magnet. It seems to be the focus for a large percentage of the miscellaneous life of the area. Is it the scavenging instinct that is strong in practically all Creation? Something for nothing? Why should partridges, for instance, haunt the tidewrack of the water's edge? And pheasants, far from the buckthorn coverts, with so much fine grassland nearby? And what is there to attract the rabbits, I wonder, that

hop about there, shaking their feet daintily when they get wet? Admittedly I do not see the hares down there often. Some of the seabirds one can understand, with gulls inveterate gleaners and scavengers. Crows likewise. And the terns, I suppose, are seeking the small fry in the shallows. The skuas, those black pirates of the sea, are hunting and harrying the others. And the waders belong to the tide's edge – the knots, the sanderling, the dunlin and the rest. But what of the others? The oyster-catchers? The curlews? The lapwings? The widgeon and mallard, the shelduck and snipe, the kittiwakes, even the woodpigeons? Are they all bitten by the same bug – the collecting bug? Or is it the other way round? Is it the bugs themselves that they are after – the myriad insects, flies and sand-hoppers that also infest the littered margin of the sea?

This brings me to the rats. It is a curious thing, but only once in all the years have I seen a live rat out here. Yet every morning the night-smoothed sand is criss-crossed by the tracks of hundreds of them, descending to the tideline. Where from? Where do they live? Soft sand-dunes are not safe for holes – too apt to cave in – and rats are shrewd creatures. Anyway, I have never seen a hole that looked like a rat-hole, in the sands, and disused rabbit-burrows quickly fall in. Seldom indeed have I come across a dead rat – and when I have it has been long dead and very bald, as though washed up by the sea itself. This is one of those mysteries, for clearly the brutes are there, somewhere, in their swarms. Not that I would have them more prominent, needless to say – for though I acknowledge a great respect for rats' intelligence, I can no more bring myself to appreciate them than can most other people. Not that they upset me, as they seem to do many folk; they have what amounts to a pathological effect on my wife, for instance. I used to keep large numbers of angora rabbits at one time, and often when I was feeding them after dark, putting my hand into the various hutches feeling for their dishes, I used to touch rats that were sitting in beside them eating their leavings. I got quite used to their little red eyes gleaming at me out of the gloom. But never was I bitten or otherwise incommoded. A lot of the stories one hears about rats are, I suspect, apocryphal.

Apocryphal or not, an old farmer friend of mine used to tell a wonderful story of the species. Like most farms, his had been much troubled by rats; particularly was his mother concerned about the stealing of eggs from that part of the steading where the hens were shut up. She blamed this on the rats, though her husband doubted if they were responsible, since exit from the stone-walled former hay-shed was difficult, all holes had been blocked up, and no egg shells were ever left. He suspected human thieves amongst the farm-workers. One night, when my friend was sitting up alone in the stable next door, with a mare about to foal, he had been almost asleep on the hay when he perceived movement up on a half-floored loft that led through from above the henhouse next door. It was made by two rats rolling an egg between them. Gently, skilfully, they steered it – and since eggs by no means roll a straight course, they had their work cut out. My friend was intrigued – but still more so in the next stage. For the loft was only half-floored, and mere narrow end-wise beams stretched across above most of the stabling. What would the rats do, what could they do, when they came to the slender joists?

The rodents had passed this way before, it seemed, however. According to my old farmer, he was astonished to see, when they got to the edge of the flooring, one of the rats turn over on its back and take the egg up on to its stomach, held in place there by its four paws. Whereupon the other took its companion's tail in its mouth, and proceed to draw carrier and egg slowly and surely across the tight-rope of the beam, a dozen feet at least, to the safety of the barn beyond. My friend always vouched for the truth of this story – even if it had happened a long long time before.

47

I have mentioned the terns along the tideline. These contribute their own mede of mysteries to the many that maintain at least my personal wonder in this enchanted territory. The terns bulk quite large in my life from June until September each year – these graceful sea-swallows, the most infuriating, bad-tempered, aggressive and restless birds in the catalogue. And the most stupid too, in one respect.

Altogether there are six varieties of tern, all of which may be seen in the Bay at one time or another – the arctic, little, sandwich, roseate, black and common terns – but it is the last with which I am mainly concerned, as regular summer residents. The tern mysteries are threefold – or perhaps four.

Firstly, why are they such fools as continuously to nest below high-water mark – and so have their eggs and chicks washed away each year with weary monotony by high tides? And a subsidiary, arising out of this – how has the species managed to survive in such notably healthy fashion if the creatures do

48

this elsewhere than at the Aberlady bar sand spit? Secondly, when they are such obviously efficient and energetic fishers, why do three-quarters of the tribe prefer to spend their boundless energy and lung-power in mobbing and attacking whichever of their number has for the moment caught a fish, in order to make it drop it – whereupon the successful bandit, catching the falling titbit in mid-air, itself becomes the target for all screaming assaults – instead of the much more simple and satisfactory procedure of diving and catching their own fish? Thirdly, why do they so demonstrably hate mankind so much, diving and swooping savagely on anyone who happens to come anywhere near them, when man is probably the least of the influences that menace their species' well-being? And all this being so – fourthly, why should the dedicated orni-thologists be so anxious to protect and preserve this ill-natured though attractive-looking fowl that is patently in no danger of dying out? Mysteries indeed.

To take the last first; at the urgent request of the ornitho-logical members of the Management Committee of the Aberlady Bay Nature Reserve, on which I have the honour to serve, we employ a part-time warden for six or eight weeks of the breeding season for no other purpose than to watch over these terns' nests and protect them from disturbance – from human beings, I may add, since even our devoted Warden cannot prevent the high tides from engulfing them, nor rats from robbing the nests at night. Nests, of course, is something of a misnomer, for the creatures do not bother to build nests, contenting themselves with scraping a brief hollow in the soft sand, or just as frequently not troubling even to do that but making use of any furrow, depression, even a man's footprint, in which to lay their eggs. In consequence, since the eggs themselves are fairly well camouflaged as to colour, it is the easiest thing in the world to trample on them, as people all unwittingly do. Hence the Warden. I suppose that boyhood's primeval urge for egg-collecting is still not wholly eradicated, despite the obedient days in which we live, so that this is a further duty for our patient watcher – not that I have heard that he is much exercised on this score. Nevertheless, precious few baby terns ever survive in Aberlady Bay to join in the great autumn migration. No large numbers actually nest, of course, despite the huge flocks of, it is calculated, up to 15,000 which assemble hereabouts in August and September. Some seasons there may be forty breeding couples, others fewer still – and three eggs is the normal clutch. Anyway, almost inevitably the high tides that we always get in midsummer wash away these ridiculously-placed eggs or helpless chicks, and we are left with perhaps ten survivors to show for our investment and the Warden's efforts. Expensive birds, these. But ornithologists are stern and unworldly folk, and not to be deflected from their chosen course.

What makes them love and esteem the terns so? I do not know. Give me an eider-duck any day, or an oyster-catcher, a kittiwake, or even a chattering red-shank. In fact, give me any fowl that does not dive screeching at my head – and does not always manage to pull away in time, either, with an inch to spare! I have been struck on the pate before now, once to the effusion of blood, and I hate to think what might happen if one rather less expert dive-bomber actually failed to put its air-brakes and flaps to work until one-thousandth of a second too late – for the brutes have notably long and sharp beaks and my head is less thickly thatched than once it was.

In their way, however, I suppose that the terns make as distinctive and authentic a contribution to the summer scene as do the crooning eiders, despite the similarity to the creaking of unoiled springs of their disgruntled cries. Their slender white bodies, little black caps, and elegant forked tails streaking across the blue of the sky; their swift vertical plunge – when they are not diving on myself – straight into the azure sea from a considerable height, setting up silvery fountains; their prompt emergence with the inevitable gleaming, wriggling sprat – and equally prompt and inevitable attack by all their wheeling companions, who prefer fish stolen to fish legitimately caught – all this is part of the summer at Aberlady Bay, and I would not be without it. When autumn comes, there is a fifth mystery. Whence do all the other terns come? Suddenly, instead of fifties and hundreds, there are thousands. Presumably this is an assembly point for the annual migration. Where can they be all summer? Experts claim that the vast majority of these birds fly in from the west, and only a few come up the coast from the east. Where have they been nesting? And were they all so much more wise in that nesting than our own local idiots, as to produce these vast flocks? Surely not – for it is not to be presumed that it is always the same unenlightened fowl that come back to Aberlady Bay and their folly? I await guidance.

Sometimes the terns encounter spectacular competition in their diving and fishing. This is when the gannets move in, the great solan geese whose dramatic diving is probably the most exhilarating sight to be seen around these coasts. There is a large and famous colony of them on the renowned Bass Rock about ten miles down the estuary, and though they do not often come up as far as Aberlady, sometimes in wild weather, or when following a shoal of fish, they appear off the Point. Then they liven things up with a vengeance – and for a while, quite a while usually, my pen is stilled.

The birds are huge, three feet and more in length, with a greenish tinge to their heads, their plumage otherwise being pure white – save for the notable black tips to their six-foot wing span. Their beaks are long and like spearheads. If any come, hundreds come, and for a mile around the sea seems to boil and seethe, with their plungings in and their burstings out again from the depths. They circle high in the air, wheeling on motionless wings, probably at least one hundred feet up,

51

then suddenly drop like a plummet, absolutely sheer and at such speed as almost to cheat the eye. High spouts the white water, and they disappear for long seconds. Then up they

spring, gulping down the fish, not carrying it about in their beaks like the terns, and spiral up and up to repeat the process. How large a quantity of fish these great birds can consume in a day I have no idea – but they appear to be as incessant at their swallowing as they are at their diving. Herrings are said to be their principal diet – but one wonders, when the herring shoals are known to have so largely disappeared from these east coast waters.

What I would like to have explained to me is the refraction problem. How do these heavy massive creatures, spotting individual fish from high in the air – deep down evidently, judging by the duration of their plunges beneath the surface – how do they manage to correct the inevitable refraction error caused by the water? Anyone who has tried to spear anything at an angle under water knows just what mystifies me. Do the gannets automatically allow for this, whatever the depth, in their initial dive? Or is it a last-instant correction made visually below the surface? In which case, dealing with so fast-moving a target as a fish in its own element, the bird's reactions must be swift beyond all measure.

Less dramatic fishers are the cormorants and shags, of which there are usually a number in our vicinity. These of course are surface divers, long streamlined spiv-like creatures with serpentine necks and rapier bills. Although as tall as the gannets, fully three feet, they are too weedy-looking and, from a distance, dingily-hued, to look very impressive – save in one favourite attitude. For some reason, cormorants and shags, alone of all sea-birds to my knowledge, feel the need to dry their wings after immersion. At least, I assume that this is the reason behind their behaviour. They are to be seen, anyway, decorating the tops of convenient posts or projecting wreckage, well out from high-water mark of course, with their great wings extended, motionless, as though carved there, for all the world like the eagle standards of lost Roman legions sunk below the waves. They will sit for hours thus – long, surely, after the said wings are dry – statuesque, evidently tireless, basking in sun or wind; and if, as in our Bay, there are many projecting poles, relics of the wartime fear of enemy aircraft landings, then the effect of a dozen or more spread-eagle totem poles can be quite fantastic, with a sort of brooding ageless dignity.

There are a couple of old midget submarines out on the middle of the bar – Italian I am told, and another relic of the war – and sometimes in lieu of a pole a cormorant will perch and display on one of these. The effect then is vastly different – quite extraordinary. The rusty and battered hulk becomes some prostrate and defeated monster, and the wide-winged creature above some victorious and avenging angel, rather like Saint Michael and the Devil. A noble tableau.

53

Less dignified and noble is another picture that I might

leave with you, concerning the cormorant. One late afternoon, on my way home, I had almost reached the footbridge
when Tess's behaviour – so often a magnet to draw my mind
from what I should be writing – attracted my attention. She
was all but twisting her head off, turning it this way and that
through fully 270 degrees, in the most evident astonishment
at what she saw. Following her pop-eyed gaze, I saw only about
thirty yards away, out on the floodtide in the Peffer mouth, a
preoccupied cormorant. I had never seen one so close inshore
nor so near the haunts of men. This cormorant was not
concerned with drying its wings, nor presenting a tableau. It
had a problem on its hands – or rather, in its long beak. It had
in fact caught a tartar, a fish, a flounder – and a large one. But
that was as far as it went. By no manner of means could it do
anything practical with that furiously flapping flat-fish. The
thing just wasn't the right shape – far too wide to swallow down
that serpentine gullet whole – twist, bend or contort as it would
both itself and the flounder. It did not seem to occur to the
cormorant to bite the annoying fish into segments with its

sharp bill and so dispose of it piecemeal. Mouthing, shaking
  and apostrophising with guttural croaks its unco-operative
catch, the bird swam round and round, in narrow circles,
achieving no solution. My heart bled for all concerned.

I never learned the outcome of this sad business, for after a
couple of minutes or so more, the cormorant started to head
out for the open sea at speed, the flounder still frantically
flapping. It occurred to me that the fowl possible reckoned
that once out in really deep water it might be able to drown the
thing.

Tess leered at me, and trotted on to the bridge.

CHAPTER FIVE

Shifting Sand and Wildfowlers

I mentioned the old Italian submarines on the bar. These, and the constant sight of the pilot-cutter out in the Forth, gave me the idea for my novel *A Drug On The Market*. Often of a winter's night, when the tide was low and I was out after the geese, I would crouch by those submarines half-buried in the sand,

hoping that they might afford me just that slight cover which would enable me to escape the keen night-sight of the wildfowl. Which they never did, I may say. Once even I got right inside the more entire of the two craft, and hunched down in the cramped little conning-tower-cum-cabin, half-filled as it was with water. I had trouble with the lid, a heavy iron affair like a rusty-hinged manhole-cover. It had been one-third open, and was very hard to make much wider. I had difficulty in inserting myself, and still more difficulty in forcing the hatch sufficiently agape to give me an upward arc of fire. I remember thinking, as I crouched there in that narrow wet iron coffin in the windy dark miles from anywhere, with the bar roaring all around me – thinking that it would be a less than pleasant fate to be trapped inside the thing, with the tide creeping in and in and up and up. Supposing the lid fell part-shut again, and could not be raised from within, hinges corroded with rust as they were? The tide, of course, covers the submarines long before high-water. There are jagged holes in the sides, caused by cannon-fire – for the captured craft were not wrecked here, but beached on the exposed bar to provide targets in a safe situation for low-flying aircraft – but none of the holes were nearly large enough to crawl through. So vivid did my imaginings become, indeed, that I presently scrambled out of the cigar-shaped hull, geese or no geese.

There was the dramatic situation, then, such as every novelist seeks for his stories. The problem now was to find a theme with which to integrate it.

The pilot-cutters out from North Berwick helped to provide this. Most days I see these sturdy craft, not much larger than the typical seine-net fishing-boats, beating up and down the estuary in all weathers, waiting to put aboard or take off the pilots on the big ships entering or leaving the Forth. Often I watched them, frequently in very rough conditions, drawing alongside the towering steel walls of giant tankers from the Middle East or the rusty flanks of tramps from the seven seas, and the hazardous transfer of nimble pilots via crazily swinging rope-ladders – and felt that there must be a story here, somewhere.

It was not until I was making my long voyage to and from Brazil, for the International PEN Congress at Rio, that it clicked. There, at numerous ports and estuaries, my liner took pilots aboard, often at night, and I was able really to grasp the elements of the procedure – the pilot-cutter winking its message out of the darkness, the great ship slowing down to a halt and switching on a searchlight to illuminate the approaching cutter, the manoeuvring alongside, amidships on the lee side, the letting down of the rope-ladder, the waiting for a suitable moment when the violently tossing small craft and the heavily heeling large one were close enough and in sufficient rhythm for the pilot to make his sometimes alarming leap from canting deck on to tossing ladder, the cutter waiting close until he was safely up and aboard the ship before it sheered off. All this might take five minutes and more – ample time for another waiting, unlighted and skilfully-handled small craft, a fishing-boat for instance, to move in on the opposite, the weather side of the ship, where no one official would be likely to be looking, and there to receive contraband goods, prohibited drugs for instance, lowered by crewmen in the racket. I never saw this happen, I must confess – but the imagination is a wonderful thing. With the far side of the ship in deep darkness, in contrast to the blaze of light illuminating the operations at the lee side, there could be smuggled into the country all sorts of things, lowered on ropes or down ladders, even illegal immigrants, before the Customs or Immigration authorities could be involved. I knew that Indian Hemp, marijuana, the drug of the teenage addicts in the United States, was coming into this country from the Middle East in increasing amounts, and worrying the authorities. Thirty thousand pounds' worth had been captured on a ship in Glasgow docks not long before. Here, then, was my story – with a perfectly safe hiding-place for the smuggled booty, stowed temporarily in the watertight compartments within the hull of the midget submarine on the Aberlady Bay bar, and menace to trap my hero therein as at last he runs the evil business to earth. Or, at least, to sand.

I have been mildly prophetic in some of my novels. Notably in *The Freebooters,* which foretold the Stone of Destiny's taking, only a couple of months before it happened; in *The Chosen Course* which foreshadowed unethical exploitation of Highland areas for hydro-electric development and financial juggling; in *Kettle Of Fish* ,which was written fully a year before the salmon drift-net war really exploded; and so on. Let us hope that *Drug On The Market* is a novel which will have no such repercussions.

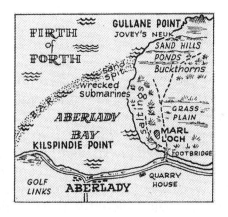

I have to admit that I did one rather mean thing in that book, which I hope will not add to anybody's little anxieties – though, of course, not everything that one writes in a novel is intended to be read as cold fact. It so happens that there is a strong local belief in Aberlady and vicinity that there are dangerous quicksands out in the Bay. How this notion came about I have no idea, for, as I have already indicated, ridiculously few of the local people ever set foot even on the Timber Bridge, much less venture out into the vast tidal reaches of the Bay. But there it is. The story is that there are deep holes in the firm sand and that these have become filled up with soft blown sand which holds the water and into which one can sink and disappear. I cannot believe that there is any truth in this. I have quartered and criss-crossed every foot of the Bay now, surely, not once but many times, in all the years, and I have never come across anything of the sort. Nor have any of my wildfowler friends. I think that we may take it as a picturesque legend, no more. I have used it in my novel, nevertheless, to heighten the tension. Allowable from a literary point of view, of course – but it would be a pity, since I am writing of a real area, if anybody was to be unnecessarily alarmed therefor.

Actually, of course, I have at least partly redeemed myself, I assert, by reassuring my readers therein as to the non-lethal habits of the tide in the Bay. I find that visitors to the area – and this no doubt refers to locals too – can be much concerned about the possibility of being cut off by the tide out on the great sand-flats. This is understandable, even sensible – but in fact no-one, birdwatcher, wildfowler or ordinary walker out on the bar need fear for his life if he will but grasp and remember a simple piece of local geography. This is that the tide does not in fact come in straight over the bar, but creeps round behind it from the west, via the mouth of the Peffer Burn. This may sound even more alarming, especially in the darkness – but it means that the bar itself, and especially the extreme eastern end of it where it becomes the sand spit, is the last to be covered of all the Bay. In other words, one can always walk out, even when the tide is swirling around one's knees in mid-Bay, merely by heading north-east – that is, towards Gullane Point. And if it is so dark that one does not know in which direction is Gullane Point or north-east, then use Inchkeith lighthouse as a beacon, putting it as it were at ten o'clock on a watch and head for two o'clock. One will find the water shallowing all the way – and the tide comes in over the levels at less than walking pace. Unfortunately this is by no means commonly realised, and I have heard of panic-stricken rushes in quite the opposite direction, straight landwards indeed, where, because the Peffer has still to be crossed, the water suddenly gets deeper and deeper. If one could look down on the Bay from an aircraft at three-quarters tide, it would be to see the entire area covered save for a long arrowhead of dry sand thrusting out from the north-east corner – a sure escape route for lingerers. This is also covered at full tide, of course – but by that time nobody should be in the Bay anyway, unless in a boat or swimming.

Footbridge to Enchantment

Despite all this, I should say that it would be quite possible for any normal-sized adult to walk out almost anywhere on the Bay, so long as he did not attempt to cross the hidden channel of the Peffer, which clings pretty close to the south and west sides – with the water coming perhaps no higher than his breast. Mind you, I have never tried it – but I do not think that it would be deeper than that. Spring tides, naturally, are a different story.

Probably it is the mud that has given Aberlady Bay its slightly alarming reputation. The Peffer Burn, which drains some of the richest farmland in the British Isles, brings down with it a great deal of top-soil, in the form of glutinous black silt. This it deposits in a belt along either side of its twisting channel through the sand-flats, never much more than one hundred yards in width, and varying in depth from the normal two or three inches to a couple of feet and more, where mussel beds have caught and held the mud. It pays to be wary of these – though they do in fact provide my favourite cover for the duck flighting at dawn and dusk; indeed they are the only cover available. The deep mud can anchor wellington-boots or waders all too effectively. I have vivid memories of seeking to extricate a friend of mine who had come wildfowling with me one winter's night, and who, injudiciously plunging forward, dragged one bare leg and foot right out of a firmly-held thigh-boot, falling flat on his face in the black slime in the process. There he lay scrabbling, unable either to raise himself up or to pull himself forward, his other leg and boot as securely embedded. A sad sight. He was in no danger, as I hurriedly shouted to him, for the sand below the couple of feet of mud was firm as a rock – but that did not seem to offer a lot of consolation. I had difficulty in aiding him, for of course whenever I lingered too long, or pressed down too heavily, on one spot, a like grip developed on my own boots. I had to keep moving, using a skating motion, ploutering around him, never

62

in exactly the same spot for more than a couple of seconds at a time, seeking to find some higher bunch of mussels underneath on which I might base my feet – whilst in a mixture of piteous wails and angry demands for succour, my cursing friend floundered in the mire. Eventually, by getting him to clasp his muddy arms around my middle, and myself leaning backwards and backwards, taking tiny but difficult steps to the rear the while, I was able to suck him out – minus both boots now. The recovery of those boots thereafter, and worse, the getting of them on to his slimy feet again, is best left undescribed. Indeed the retrieving of the gun, which had completely disappeared into the mud, was also quite something, and its eventual cleaning. A bonny pair we looked at the end of it, I can assure you. My wife's comments when we arrived at the house thus may be omitted likewise. The ducks undoubtedly laughed last that night – as indeed they are apt to do.

I may say that I used this incident in the novel likewise, changing the sex of the victim – a device which of course permitted all sorts of suitable refinements and interesting developments, as one may imagine if one is that way inclined.

That mud made a profound impression once upon our national Press. It was at the time of the famed Aberlady Bay affair in 1953, when I was fighting to prevent the area being turned into a Nature Reserve – not because of any ill-will towards nature reserves as such, but solely because, amongst other restrictions and by-laws, this one was going to ban duck-shooting; and wildfowling below the high-water mark is in Scotland one of the common law rights of the citizen. But that is an old story. What matters here is that I had announced to the world that on the first day of that shooting season, with two other wildfowlers, I was going to challenge the said by-laws by shooting at ducks, if any presented themselves – and the Pressmen presented themselves in large numbers to see the fun. As did the police, militant ornithology and the general public. It was a stirring occasion, even though no ducks showed up – understandably, since the Bay was never so thronged before or since.

But the Press, unfortunately, had underestimated the mud. Indeed, I suppose that most of them did not even know that there was any mud. This applied to the police too, I may say – but I did not feel the same responsibility for them, somehow. For one thing, the journalists, unlike the law, all turned up at my house before the battle started, and were fed with coffee and biscuits in order to get them into a suitably biased good humour. Alas, for what was to follow! When I perceived the footwear in which the Fourth Estate planned to follow me out into the Bay, apprehension was born in me, I must confess. Only one, as I recollect, of seven or eight reporters and four photographers, had thought to bring wellington-boots. Not even galoshes or any sort of over-shoes were in evidence. My warnings were laughed off by the tough Pressmen. Our own establishment was ransacked for footwear more apt to the occasion – but with scant success, for so large an invasion, not unnaturally. Consequently, in due course, as the dusk began to fall, down to the Bay after me trooped many pairs of natty city shoes, in gleaming calf, spotless suede and the like.

At first, the firm sand seemed to belie my warnings, and all was gaiety. Then gradually the skin of mud superimposed – and deepened and thickened. Heart-rending were the cries, dramatic the curses. But it was too late to turn back. Duty called, and the story is everything to devoted professionals. More than one, against my advice, took off shoes and socks and rolled up trouser-legs above formerly white calves. I remember painfully the little red coiling worms of blood which one representative of a large-circulation daily left behind him on the black mud surface, from bare feet cut by the razor-sharp edges of buried mussel-shells. My respect for the gallant gentlemen of the Press went up that night by leaps and bounds

– even though one was heard to remark to an unsympathetic birdwatcher that even if Tranter didn't manage to shoot a duck, at least he had heard that there was believed to be a black-tailed goblin or something of the sort in the Bay, and wasn't this rather rare? The presumption that he meant a bar-tailed godwit was never actually proved.

Incidentally the eventual outcome of our long fight in the Bay – it went on for three years, fowlers getting charged and the charges dropped, and charged again – was that our case was upheld by the Sheriff in the County Court. However, the Crown sadly – that is, the Government under another name – appealed against the Sheriff's judgement, and the three learned Appeal Court judges, two of whom were ex-Solicitors-General, reversed the judgement in favour of the reigning Solicitor-General, who led against us. They agreed that the Sheriff might be right as far as Scots Law was concerned, but held that since the supreme court of Parliament had in its wisdom declared, even as an afterthought, that the legislation under which the Aberlady Nature Reserve was set up – The National Parks and Access to the Countryside Act 1949 – should also apply to Scotland, its august wish must prevail. Irrespective of Scots Law, presumably. Well, well – not for me to criticise my betters . . .

So there is Aberlady Bay Local Nature Reserve, and fires may not be lit for picnics, wild flowers must not be pulled by bairns, nor tadpoles caught. Duck are now only to be shot on permit from the Management Committee – which is somewhat embarrassing for me as a member thereof. However the duck taste much the same thus, roasted, as heretofore. The wild geese, unfortunately, are a vexed question.

Something was lost, I feel, out of that prolonged struggle, something important. Or am I just being old-fashioned?

CHAPTER SIX

Hunting and Harrying

Tess, I think, likes everything across the bridge, wet or fine, summer or winter, things animate or inanimate, smells of every sort, wide spaces to bound in, curious places to explore, freedom. She is even more consistently enchanted than I am myself, I suppose. Except by the owls.

Tess does not like the owls, that is certain. Owls, out here you see, behave in the same topsy-turvy fashion as does most of the rest of nature. Elsewhere they are usually considered to be unobtrusive night-hunters, silent save when they hoot. Beyond the footbridge, however, they change all that. They hunt by day. They become bold, aggressive. They make screaming and barking noises. And they never hoot or toowit-toowoo – or at least, I have never heard them do so.

It may be just that short-eared owls are different from other owls, of course. There is nearly always one pair, and frequently two, hunting the grass plain, year in, year out. I presume that they nest in the buckthorns at the Marl Loch, or thereabouts – large powerful birds, swift on the wing however heavy-flapping they seem. Fierce hunters, they have no fear of man – and certainly none of Tess. In fact, I don't think that they fear anything; they give that impression. And it is noteworthy that I never see them being mobbed, like the kestrels and the sparrowhawks, the crows, and even the skuas, by swarms of small birds, by terns and peewits. Perhaps, of course, they do not threaten these others, or their eggs, and are only interested in mice, frogs and suchlike.

However that may be, they are distressingly interested in Tess. Poor creature, if they are anywhere about then she gets no peace from them. They follow her, swooping and diving on her, harrying her from pillar to post – or at least from reed-clump to buckthorn – screeching and threatening. Tess, I think, is not so much frightened as embarrassed. Obviously she deplores them utterly, slinking along with her ears, head, and tail down, in unaccustomed fashion, seeking to make herself as small as may be, forever casting outraged glances, not upwards but back at me. I have not seen her actually struck by one of these owls, though she may well have been buffeted by their wide and powerful wings. She never seems to snap back at them, however – though she does when peewits occasionally swoop on her, and her leaping up at the larks has already been mentioned. Is she just an abject coward then, cringing before the big stuff but bold enough with the small?

There may be something of that in it, for few dogs of my acquaintance are really of the stuff of heroes. But I feel that there is more to it than that. Those owls are queer brutes. Unchancy is the word, perhaps. You see, I know something of how Tess feels – for they give me a certain amount of the same treatment. There is something distinctly off-putting, to say the least of it, to be walking along in the middle of nowhere, with a curious presence floating immediately above you, perhaps four feet above, utterly silent as to propulsion, staring down at you with a pair of huge round side-by-side eyes, unwinking, expressionless, yet somehow baleful, occasionally making a throaty screech at you. When this goes on and on, it can come between man and his work, or a dog and its self-esteem. Nearly all birds have strange staring eyes – but owls are quite the strangest, I think.

The mobbing of predators by numbers of those whom they oppress individually is, of course, common practice, sound tactics, and poetic justice into the bargain. I am all for it. Strangely enough, it seems to be a bird habit rather than an animal one. Apart from man himself – who doesn't do nearly as much of it as good sense would seem to indicate – I cannot think for the moment of any other of the animal kingdom who make a habit of such salutory action against the gangsters and the bullies. Who has ever heard of a flock of mice mobbing a weasel? Or a bevy of rabbits chasing a fox? It may be, of course, that the animals seldom bunch together as do the birds, and therefore have no means of working up a united front. Yet where they do tend to congregate, they still do not go in for mobbing. Herds of caribou have no idea of harrying one of the wolves that attack them, effectively as they could do so, with sharp hooves and horns. And our own herds of red deer never turn on the eagles which attack the calves – however stoutly a single hind may on occasion lash out to defend her own young. I have heard that squirrels will occasionally mob certain enemies – or just other squirrels. But squirrels are too much of a rarity in my experience for checking on such reports. Our indigenous red squirrel is certainly not a gregarious character, moreover.

I do not know whether any of the insect kingdom can be said to go in for mobbing. Possibly not. Hunting as a pack, perhaps – but that is not the same thing. They then become the predators. Or do they? What, for instance, of the time when, halfway out to the sand-hills, I observed an ordinary white cabbage butterfly behaving in a definitely extraordinary fashion? The creature was not fluttering about in the sunshine in normal light-hearted style, but darting up and down, to and fro, at great speed and in most evident agitation. I left the path to investigate this – and found that the unfortunate butterfly was being mobbed by a host of tiny black flies. They were attacking it most determinedly. My eye caught another flutter perhaps a hundred yards away, and there the same procedure was being repeated. There may have been many such encounters scattered over the plain. I had never noticed anything of the sort before, however normal a matter your expert lepidopterist might consider it. Now, which were the predators in this case? Do these flies prey on butterflies? Or is it the other way round, and are our pretty and harmless flutterers in fact Jekyll and Hyde killers of small fry, which here were just getting some of their own back?

I must admit that I quite enjoy watching a really good-going mobbing, a bully having caught a pack of tartars, a tough being cut down to size. Such sights promptly read me practical lessons on what we should all do about our domineering politicians, overbearing bureaucrats, petty dictators, trade union bosses, and aggressive delinquents generally. Most would be the sweeter for a good mobbing at regular intervals. As when the savage snooping black skuas take a beating from a score of furiously screaming terns; or a trio of side-slipping aerobatic peewits go tooth and nail for a lean and hungry hawk, or a flock of finches deal effectively with a nest-raiding hoodie crow. Undoubtedly there is a place in the scheme of things for all these predators – a quite important place – just as there is for those who know exactly how we should be governed, controlled and directed. The All Wise made them as they are, presumably, and it is not for us to think to improve upon His handiwork. When we start trying, we usually end up with a pretty intricate mess, however good our intentions. As I have tried to indicate. Nevertheless, the said bully-boys have to be kept in their place. It doesn't do to let them get out of hand – the Big Brothers, the bosses, the batterers. Nature provides a series of checks and balances. Mankind, it seems to me, especially in this age of uniformity and conformity, is less clever.

Perhaps these are merely the thoughts of an outdated rebel?

This, I can well believe, is where some of my birdwatcher friends chip in. Just listen to the man, I can hear them say! Isn't he a predator himself, a killer, a self-condemned slaughterer of defenceless birds? A wildfowler, in fact. I have had that said to me, and in no uncertain terms – one anonymous letter told me to go and shoot myself, murderer, instead of the said defenceless birds – often enough to have given the matter some consideration. Man *is* a predator, of course – the most insistent and universal of all the predators. He is a carnivore, and unless we all turn vegetarian forthwith, we are in no position to deplore it. But this is mere generalising, I agree. Why do I shoot wildfowl for pleasure, is the real question, undoubtedly – for I will not pretend that I would starve otherwise. Although I do indeed only shoot fowl that my household or my friends may eat.

First of all, I suppose that it must be accepted that the hunting instinct is fairly strongly implanted within me. Probably indeed it is in most actively-minded men – though the majority may turn it into other channels; the pursuit of money, of power, of collections of various sorts – or just of women! Allowing this, I would say that it is probably the challenge implicit in wildfowling that holds me in thrall. For it is a very real challenge. A less easy, convenient, and materially rewarding pastime would be hard to find – with the exception perhaps of deerstalking, my other love. That is, in sports where the object is to collect something. When I point out that last year my total bag for well over twenty sallies into the Bay was five ducks, something of the potency of the challenge may be grasped. Though I agree this was a particularly poor season.

All sorts of shooting present some challenge, of course – even if only the challenge of marksmanship on a moving target. But that is not what I mean – for I must confess that the idea of waiting in a butt or hide and shooting driven grouse or pheasants does not much appeal to me, however much gunmanship and skill may be called for. The wildfowler pits his wits and enthusiasm against a variety of vastly greater challenges than these – in Aberlady Bay, at any rate. For one thing the sport has to be pursued in the darkness, or if fortunate, in the three-quarters dark, for that is when the duck flight. One does not stalk or hunt ducks; not in shore-shooting, where there is no cover for ducks or shooter. It can only be done at dusk or dawn, when the fowl are on their swift way to or from their feeding grounds. They are sharp-eyed creatures, with infinitely better night vision than have humans, and since there is nothing to hide behind out on the mud-flats, the chances of them coming within range at all, on any but a really dark night are very low. The aforementioned mussel-beds do not actually provide cover – they only help to break up the outline, and make it less obviously a man. Even so, the beds reaching no more than two feet in height, it is only on the very blackest night that a wildfowler may remain standing. And sitting in this deep mud, whether on an old oil-drum, a shooting-stick or just on a semi-submerged gamebag – or again, lying out flat on the firmer wet sand, often with an inch or more of surface water on top – for hours of a wild winter's night, is not everyone's idea of fun.

The advantages are all with the ducks, then – except, I admit, that they cannot shoot back! Perhaps they get their own back indirectly through the wildfowler's colds, rheumatism, and varied frustrations. For they flight too high to be shot in fine or calm weather, so that it is in gales, driving rain or snow, or sometimes in thick mist, that they come low enough for shooting with a twelve-bore shotgun – the effective range of which is not more than forty yards against a strongly-quilled bird like a duck. These conditions ensure maximum inconvenience and minimum bags. Nor are the birds in any way predictable in their habits, and there is no guarantee that the shivering marksman will so much as get a single shot. The majority of nights that I go out, indeed – and I seldom go in for the dawn flighting, though it is apt to be more profitable, being over-fond of my bed at such times – no shot is fired at all. Duck may be about, and usually are, but as I have explained, they have to be very close to be heard, much less shot.

Heard is the operative word, for the actual shooting has to be done by ear and instinct rather than by sight. The fowler fires at movement rather than at a bird – the impression of movement in something that is only slightly darker than the night's darkness above. Movement which, in the mallard, my main target, is reckoned to be as fast as sixty-five miles an hour – more, down-wind. Which means that I do not really fire at the actual movement either, but quite a bit ahead of it. Which as perhaps you will perceive is no simple matter. Two ducks ahead of a duck is the favoured formula – which might be all right if one could see the original duck in the first place. Even when I do actually see the shape of the bird for an instant, as sometimes happens, it is seldom for long enough to line up my gun, calculate aim-off, initiate the follow-through movement, and press the trigger. So that we are back to shooting by instinct and hearing.

The hearing is vitally important – for the whistle and beat of pinions is the only warning that I get. On a dark and blustery night, the hearing has to be very well developed and attuned in order to decide in which direction the fowl are coming, and therefore in which to stare in the hope of sensing their movement. Usually it is necessary swiftly to decide with myself which ear is receiving the sound. This may sound laughable, but it is literally true. Unless I am facing directly towards or away from the oncoming birds, one ear or the other does receive the vibrations of wings first and most clearly – although clear is hardly the phrase to apply to anything in the buffeting windy dark. This is the only clue proffered, and must be utilised. Even so, four out of five of the throbbings and beatings that my ears faintly pick up I never actually place. Tess is useful in this, having better ears than I have. Often by watching the direction of her cocked head, I get that precious hint of direction and angle which gives me at least a chance.

Unfortunately this is about all that she is good for, save to act as company for me out in the benighted vacancy. She will not retrieve, and has no least interest in a duck once it is dead. She has a magnificent nose, and goes bounding off enthusiastically to find anything that I bring down – but having found it, she loses all further interest and does not wait for me to come up with her but comes trotting back to me. Which is not a great help, when I am floundering about in the darkness trying to find a dark object in black mud. Nothing will teach her to lead me through the gloom to where my quarry lies – and which she can trace with the greatest of ease. Her attitude certainly would not please the profound bird-lovers any more than it pleases me. It seems to be – that's fine; that one's dead. Now – get on with the killing! I can only imagine that she thinks ducks are my deadly enemies, and that once I have disposed of one, that is all that matters. Poor Tess – she has in fact all the wrong ideas about the business, and years of teaching and coaxing, patient and otherwise, have made no impression on her.

That she so loves to come wildfowling with me is strange – for to sit for hours in the cold wet mud, shivering like a jelly, and so seldom to have anything to do, even to make a mistake about, must be boring in the extreme. Yet as soon as dusk begins to fall, from late October onwards, she is all on her toes, peering and nudging at me, waiting at the door, pointing to the cupboard where my rubber thigh-boots are kept. And when I actually pick up the gun she goes crazy with excitement and delight. Extraordinary that a creature so keen, so interested should so consistently get it all wrong. Presumably her heterogeneous ancestry is just too much for her – a crazy mixed-up cur. As the gundog of the President of the East Lothian Wildfowlers Association she is something of an embarrassment. As well that wildfowling is of all sports the most lonely.

It occurs to me that all this has rambled far from being any explanation of why I, who can enjoy seeing the predators harried for a change, can yet enjoy shooting poor defenceless fowl that never did me a bit of harm. Or perhaps not? Perhaps the perspicacious reader will have gleaned plenty from the foregoing, more than the mere words convey? Perhaps he will have his answer, after all – or more likely she, being the more intuitive, the more perceptive reader-between-the-lines. It is a fatal mistake to underestimate one's readers.

CHAPTER SEVEN

Flights of Freedom and Threats of Flooding

I have been talking about the wild duck – the mallard, widgeon, teal and the like, that flight at dusk and dawn in the Bay, or over it. The wild geese are a very different story, though of course superficially they have their similarities. It is surprising, too, how many people confuse them – especially as the geese make so unmistakable an impact on this entire seaboard, from October until March. Nobody, however housebound, however ignorant of wild life, however uninterested, can fail to be aware of their presence. For the great skeins of the geese, long rippling ribbons in the air, go honking their V-shaped way overhead, trumpeting their wild music, morning and evening, often seeming to fill the entire sky, both with their presence and their exciting challenge. None can ignore them, surely, for unlike the ducks that slip over almost in darkness, in twos and threes and small groups, with only the whisper of wings and an occasional chuckle to announce them, the geese flight in their hundreds and thousands, plain for all to see, earlier in the evening and later in the morning. Indeed sometimes all through the day, coming and going, when the moon is full and they can feed by night.

Their habits, in fact, reverse those of the ducks. The latter feed by night on the inland stubbles and water-meadows, and lie out on the bosom of the sea all day, asleep. The geese feed by day, particularly on the farmers' precious winter wheat, and come out to the sand-bar at night to rest and preen.

These are pink-footed geese almost entirely – although occasionally a few of greylag or brent are to be identified amongst the others. Numbers fluctuate throughout the season and year by year, but there are often as many as five or six thousand in the Bay, of a winter. And numbers like that, of such large, energetic and vocal birds as these, make no small impression, willy-nilly, on any neighbourhood that they haunt.

Any calm winter night when the wind is not booming loudly to swallow all, the sound with which we go to sleep in Quarry House is the high-pitched incessant gabble, honk, and bugling of thousands of lusty throats over a mile away out on the sands, rising against and above the steady thunder of the seas on the bar itself. A good sound that, I suppose, that few other houses in the land could offer us. We never tire of it, anyway – nor of the fluting, haunting passage-notes as the vast self-disciplined formations beat overhead by day or by moonlight. After all these years the sound can still thrill us, and we can scarcely forbear to rush out of the house to stare up at those vehement voyagers. Indeed the first hearing of the geese music each autumn is always a red-letter day, and the sound seldom fails to bring lumps to our throats.

What is it about the wild geese? They are no more than large waterfowl, after all – and their tame brethren are scarcely romantic creatures. Yet these wild ones universally seem to grip the imagination, to cast a spell, to stir something within all but the most prosaic and blasé, as does no other bird. They seem to be the very epitome of freedom, of the untamed, speaking to us of far untrodden places, of boundless empty territories and the primeval wilderness, of questing for something utterly unconstrained, independent, striking some chord that deep within us all, even the most earthbound and unadventurous, answers back incoherently but surely. Sentimental nonsense, some may say – but then, the same charge can be hurled at nearly all of those things that stir us most, from our faith, our loyalty, our patriotism, to our support of some football team.

In their own right, of course, and without any psychological delving or metaphysics, the wild geese demand our tribute. The sight of a beautifully exact V-formation of these great birds, each nearly three feet long, with a graceful wing-span of twice that length, beating with powerful rhythmic ease, long necks outstretched and the sun glinting on innumerable pale breasts, is one that is not readily forgotten.

The same old query is asked of me. How can I shoot birds that so attract and affect me? I suppose that it is begging the question to say that it is geese in the mass, the idea of the great adventuring skeins, rather than the individual fowl, which attracts me – the geese not the goose. Or is that sheer sophistry? I can see the wild geese as a symbol – and at the same time, the Pinkfoot itself as a notable and worthy quarry. Is that hopelessly inconsistent? Such a quarry they are, at any rate, for they are still harder to shoot than the ducks, super-wary and higher flying. Indeed they are in but little danger from the shore-shooter. The only way to try to get them, in the Bay, is to lie flat out on the farthest bar itself, when the tide is out, hoping to appear to them like a piece of driftwood, and trust that the geese will fly directly overhead as they come in to roost – a monumental improbability, since they do not come in slantwise, but spiral and sideslip down from a great height on to sand that they have already prospected from above – and there is an area of over two miles long by a mile wide in which they may come down anywhere. One has to be exactly beneath them, at this alighting, for a shot. Moreover, so well armour-plated are they that I have actually heard my shotgun pellets rattle off their quills – so that twenty to twenty-five yards is the maximum effective range. Need I say more? Save to add that

77

if I manage to bag two or three geese in any season, I am a proud man.

The Management Committee of the Nature Reserve decides at the beginning of each shooting season whether or not geese may be shot. Most seasons the verdict is in the negative – which may seem less than reasonable, considering that there are infinitely more geese than there are ducks, and there is no suggestion of any overall diminution of the species.

The farmers do not love the geese, I am afraid. What a few thousand large and heavy birds can do, descending upon a field of winter wheat, is no joke. Not only do they eat it back, so that a field that was solidly green in the morning can be bare black earth by afternoon; but thousands of wide, webbed feet puddling about in wet weather can so churn up the tilth that nothing will be left to grow thereafter. The East Lothian grain growers cherish no illusions about this, and many more geese are shot from the cover of field hedges or walls than ever fall to the shore-shooter's gun. But even so they are hard to bring down, for wherever the phrase 'a stupid goose' arose, these are wise birds and know all about hedges and guns. Almost invariably a keen-eyed scout surveys the area before they come in. Then they spiral down into the centre of the field instead of planing in over the hedges. Thereafter a sentinel is always on the watch from some vantage-point for gunners who may creep and stalk.

I wish that I knew more about the geese. Indeed that goes for practically everything that I see and watch out over my bridge. I am only too well aware of my ignorance of so much that it would be a delight and a satisfaction to know – in the realm of nature as in other spheres. I am afraid that I carry my tideline predilection, for picking up bits and pieces, into the wider provinces which include my belated acquisition of knowledge.

I would like to know, for instance, why it is all pinkfooted geese that come to Aberlady Bay now, when, according to the records and the experts, it was noted as a haunt of the bean goose until the late 19th century when the pinkfoot began to appear. Now bean are seldom seen here. With such vast numbers involved, this seems extraordinary. It is not as though the various sub-species of geese cannot stand each other; they all seem to mix together fairly well. What sent the bean thousands away elsewhere, and brought the pinkfoot thousands in their place?

The same applies, to a lesser extent, to the brent goose, a somewhat smaller variety. It was traditionally abundant on the East Lothian coast each winter, though numbers apparently began to fall off during the first quarter of this century. Now it is rare here, indeed. Personally I have never seen one.

I would like to know why, with such a gregarious bird, occasionally a lone goose is left behind in the Bay when all the others have gone inland to feed, and flies honking and complaining round and about the tidelands all day in sorrowful fashion. This happens quite frequently. Are these birds that have lost their mates, from some cause or other? Or are they outcasts, driven from the great flocks? They could hardly be lost. They must know their way to the feeding grounds perfectly well, since they have been going back and forwards every morning and evening hitherto. Or are they just awkward characters being difficult, and very vocal about it? One thing is certain – they are not misplaced juveniles birds so young that they do not know the form, and have somehow overslept or otherwise got left behind; for of course the geese breed in the far northern Arctic wastes, and to be here at all must be some six months old and have flown many thousands of miles.

A characteristic of the geese – our geese, at any rate – is their consistent fondness for the bar as a refuge. This is perfectly understandable of course when the tide is out, for it constitutes a sanctuary that cannot be approached unseen, flat as a billiard-table, with nothing projecting higher than a piece of driftwood – and the submarines. But when the tide is in, strangely enough, the geese seem to be just as faithful to the place, to be just as happy to sit floating *over* the bar as to stand sleeping on it. This is the more peculiar in that the bar, when covered, by its very nature is far from the calmest stretch of water to be found. It is a barrier, a wide sand barrier, and therefore inevitably even calm seas break there – the sort of place where troubled waters are always to be looked for, as anyone who knows the sea understands. Yet here the geese flocks come to rest, vast numbers of birds – when there are a hundred more sheltered areas available. Shelter, presumably, is not what they seek. As for security, any area of water, open water, would be equally safe.

Only in a full-scale storm will the geese deign to make any gesture towards the shelter of the land. In a Force Eight or Nine wind, in driving rain, sleet or snow, you will still see them battling their way out to their extraordinary choice of rest area. But I *have* seen them, very occasionally, settle in around one of the winter-time lochans amongst the sand-hills. This would be, presumably, when there was a full north-westerly gale. In such conditions, Aberlady Bay becomes a shocking place. In that direction, the nearest substantial shelter is the Highland Line behind Stirling – and that is scant help. The shape and placing of the Bay give it fairly good protection from most winds – but north-westerly it is wide open, as good as a funnel. Fortunately it is not an airt that normally gives us severe storms in these parts. When it does, even the geese have second thoughts. I have seen the Bay so full of driven spume, whipped off the surface of tossing white water, that it was impossible to see across the Timber Bridge. I have seen the line of waves away out at the bar, the tide being out, so high as to look like a great white wall, even two miles off, barring off the entire Bay – and the noise like an artillery barrage, seeming to shake the very ground. In such conditions Quarry House, at the very head of the Bay, the neck of the funnel, cowers behind its protective screen of groaning tortured trees, a single-storeyed house low-set at any time, but now crouching lower and thankful for its high wall – that other times we deplore because of the view it denies us seawards.

When it really does get alarming is when a north-westerly gale coincides with a full moon and a high spring tide. Then is the time to watch out. Great masses of water pile up in the Bay, driven in by wind and tide – and Quarry House is not more than a foot or so above sea-level – if that. The sea has been in on it before now – once, I believe, in the previous tenant's time; and local stories speak of many such occasions earlier. Indeed, I was most solemnly warned against coming to this house in the first place, by Aberlady worthies, when we moved from our house in the village itself. Fortunately the main road which runs between us and the Bay, on its slight embankment, was raised nearly a foot some years ago. And recently a further camber has been added at the seaward side – in the interests of speed, of course, not land conservation – which gives us those precious extra few inches. For the house is some feet below the level of the road, and when we see the footbridge covered and wave-crests lipping over on to the tarmacadam – then we pray for a change of wind, and keep our fingers crossed.

There was one day, a few winters ago, when things were really touch-and-go – at the time of the disastrous flooding down in East Anglia and elsewhere. The quarry from which our establishment takes its name is situated a bare hundred yards landward of the house, and is a mediaeval one – from which the pre-Reformation Priory of Luffness, and no doubt the still earlier castle, were built – not dug out of the side of a hill as is the modern fashion, but excavated from the flat ground. It is now a long deep trench, surrounded by a pine wood, into which much field drainage is led, it in turn being drained into the Bay by a culvert which runs under our garden. There is precious little fall in level between the quarry and the sea, and quite frequently at high tides the flow is reversed and the level of water in the quarry rises notably. On this well-remembered occasion, the sea seemed to be positively pumping itself into the quarry, and the level rose and rose ominously, with the natural land-drainage, strong anyway on account of a spell of wet weather, being dammed back in its turn. We had vivid visions of the flood attacking us from the rear as well as the front, in a pincers movement. It was a daunting thought. Happily, the crisis time passed, with some inches to the good, and we were spared.

It was during this same couple of days that conditions at Jovey's Neuk itself were such as I have never seen paralleled. It was a major battle, needless to say, to get out there at all – but I had to go. My son and friend likewise. The scene as we neared the Point is not to be forgotten. Spume like thick fog blew half-a-mile inland, and as we pushed our way closer to the headland, leaning at a 45-degree angle into the gale, it was like walking into a snowfield. Moving snow. The snow was however a deep layer of foam and froth creeping inland over the grass and bents like a moving carpet, large globules and great bubbles rolling and bounding fast on top. The wide sand beaches flanking the Point on the west had disappeared completely, and the ravening waves were gouging great bites out of the sand-hills, with new corries yawning here, cornices toppling there, and everywhere avalanches of loose sand hurtling down, partly blowing away like smoke in the process and partly being spewed up again by the boiling seas. Gullane Point itself, which normally projects its snout some twenty or more feet above the tide, was only intermittently to be seen, so high was the general level of the storm-banked waters. Huge individual waves broke and ran far up the grass slopes that reach up from the rocks; and the whereabouts of the normal iron-bound coastline to the east of it was only to be traced by the endless succession of tall spouts and gouts of white water that soared into the air, and were thereupon vaporised, as though laid down by an incessant naval barrage. The noise was deafening.

We went as near as we dared, and threw ourselves down, battered and breathless. I wondered what had happened to the eiders. Presumably they had headed well out to sea, and were riding it out in deep water.

It was astonishing, weeks after, to view this crazy tideline, marked by miscellaneous wrack and debris, high up on the hillside, far from the water's edge.

We had to go home the long way round, that day, for even the hand-rail of the footbridge was submerged. The bridge itself was damaged, its deep-sunk foundation piles wrenched out in two places as it were by the roots, and the planking twisted, gapped and broken.

For some weeks thereafter, until the bridge could be repaired, the road to enchantment started with quite a hop, skip and jump for Tess and myself.

CHAPTER EIGHT

The Belligerent Swan

Country people, I have found, by and large are by no means so much more knowledgeable about wildlife than are the greatly despised townies – as witness the very general mistaking of wild geese for ducks. Even more to be wondered at is the quite widespread confusion between geese and swans. Aberlady Bay can very frequently show a few wild swans, of both the mute

and whooper varieties. They are restless creatures, and though they do not flight to and from inland pastures like the geese and ducks, but remain more or less in the Bay area, they nevertheless do fly around quite a lot, in pairs or small family groups, never very high and always drawing considerable attention to themselves. For one thing, they often fly low over the village itself, just skimming the roofs, and their heavy droning wing-beats turn everyone's eyes upwards. Thereafter people will stop me and tell me, even in midsummer, that the geese are back again, or that the geese seem to be flying much lower this year, or are otherwise distinguishing themselves. Admittedly the swans are also large birds with long out-thrust necks – but there the resemblance ends, surely? Pure white where the geese are grey-brown – although the cygnets and immature birds may be mottled – they are very much larger, with longer and more serpentine necks, and their flight is much heavier, ponderous, with its distinctive sound of wind harping through powerful wing-tips.

Perhaps it is to Aberlady's credit that, modestly, all its swans are geese?

The reverse situation can apply of course. Once I was summoned to a neighbour's house to 'come and do something about a swan that has landed in our garden'. Incidentally, why people should appeal to such as myself so frequently, complete strangers as often as not, 'phoning me and calling at the house, to deal with anything that seems to them unusual in the bird line, I have never quite managed to fathom; I would have thought that a notorious wildfowler and self-confessed killer would be the last one to turn to? Anyway, on this occasion, I found that the 'swan' was a fairly young pinkfoot goose that seemed to have taken a fancy to our friend's garden – but not to the household, by any means, for it hissed and made threatening gestures whenever anyone approached, though making no attempt to fly away again. This was very unusual, of course, for normally the geese come no nearer to the haunts of men than some hundreds of feet in the air. This one did not appear to be injured in any way, or visibly ill, and the garden being a walled one, it had in fact flown in. Anyway, my own efforts to persuade it to move on were no more successful than the lady's own. The creature merely stalked about, down at the foot of the long garden, apparently contented enough until anyone came too near, when it looked hostile and tough. I ascertained that it had no marking-ring on its leg – for if it had been a ringed bird, that might have explained a certain predilection for human habitation if not human company.

Our friend, who had two young children not so very much larger than the goose itself, and who of course were fascinated by this new arrival, suggested that I should shoot it – for she feared that the creature might attack and injure the youngsters, who would not keep their distance. But though I will go to great lengths and ridiculous discomforts to try to shoot a goose out on a dark and windy sand-bar, I somehow could not find it in me deliberately and cold-bloodedly to take a gun to this dignified, pacing fowl in somebody's back garden. Foolish and inconsistent, I have no doubt – for this bird was at least upsetting a household by its unnatural performance. Perhaps it was largely a reluctance to bring the entire village about my ears by letting off a loudly banging twelve-bore shotgun in the confined space of a group of back gardens? At any rate, I made weak and feeble excuses, recommended patience and a waiting game, and fled the scene. Any credit that I had undoubtedly received a severe scaling down that day.

A true swan featured in another incident nearer home. One day, when I was out over the bridge as usual, a lady who lives nearby called at our house, concerned. She had been passing in her car, it appeared, and had had to draw up for a swan which was pacing about the road outside our gate. She and a friend, esteeming the great bird to be in danger from passing traffic, had got out and sought to herd it down from the road into the saltings of the Bay. In this they had been notably unsuccessful, however, the swan always insisting on marching back towards the Quarry House gate. The soft-hearted lady now wondered whether my wife would mind if she was to let it into our ground – we have a certain amount of rough grass with trees, as well as the more formal garden – for she feared that there would be an accident if the creature remained out on the busy road. My wife, although always one who appreciated swans at a distance rather than close up, could hardly refuse this request, and accompanied the lady back towards the gate – our house being one that turns its back on road and sea.

However, the swan had meantime taken the matter a step further, and was in fact coming stalking down the short drive towards them as they rounded the house – it presumably having flown over the five-bar gate. The second lady was looking after it, from the road, rather helplessly. There did not seem to be a lot more that could be done, or said, in the circumstances – so the motorists made vaguely hopeful noises, climbed into their car, and drove away. The Tranters had acquired a swan.

From the first moment, it seemed, the brute took up a masterful and authoritative attitude, a full-grown mute swan of major proportions and determined character. Ignoring my less than confident wife altogether, it strode on down the drive, turned to go right-about round the house, and headed unhesitatingly into our little back court. My wife, prudently, went the other way, and let herself in at the front door.

The noise started almost immediately – crash, clatter, bang! Two outhouses and a woodshed open off that back court, filled with miscellaneous gear, and there is moreover a corner for pails, ash-cans, empty-tins bin, and the like. That swan went about exploring the possibilities of all this in thorough, not to say vehement, fashion. Over went each receptacle and out spilled its contents. Doors were pushed wide, stacked implements, brushes and so on, scattered, hanging things knocked

87

off their hooks. Nothing was too heavy or bulky for that massive fowl; nothing too high for its long snake-like neck to reach; nothing too tightly closed to withstand the attacks of its powerful beak.

Although entirely catholic in its investigations, the creature kept coming back to the collection of empty tins – bugbear of any country house in this canister age. My wife, watching all this from the glass panels of the back door, concluded that hunger must be the spur. She produced some bread crusts. These the swan came for without hesitation, and snatched up roughly, dipped and douched them disgustedly in the water of Tess's bowl, spilling most of it, and then gulped down – to thrust out wide beak and coiling neck for more, imperatively, threateningly, making rude sounds the while. Indeed, from first to last, this was no genteel bird.

When the supply of bread ran out, my wife had to shut the door hurriedly or the thing would have been into the house.

Thereafter an approximate state of siege developed. The swan roamed round the house making frustrated and angry noises, while the mistress thereof went to ground and tried telepathy and wishful thinking.

After some hours of this the swan seemed to decide that there was little profit in it, and set off across the pasture field known as the Cow Park, which lies between Quarry House and the village. From a window its waddling but apparently quite decided progress was watched thankfully. My wife was prepared to let somebody else have a share in the fowl – the policeman, for instance, for whose establishment it seemed to be making a beeline.

Alas, half-an-hour later there was a rapping on the back door – and there was the swan back again, more impatient than ever and evidently peckish after its walk. When knocking thus produced no results, it took the door-handle in its beak and rattled it – an imperious bird.

My wife went to the furthest away room in the house, and tried to think of other things.

Just when the creature moved off for the second time she did not know. But, after quite a while, a cautious survey revealed no sign of it – a matter for major relief. Mrs T was not quite finished with her visitor yet, however. Presently the telephone rang, and an aggrieved voice announced that there seemed to be a very large bird, possibly some sort of goose, walking up and down the village street and interfering with the traffic and the lieges. Would Mr Tranter come along and cope with it, please?

My wife never told me the exact terms in which she replied to this caller.

It was a couple of days later before I personally became involved with this notable and peripatetic fowl. Another telephone call, this time from Gullane, informed me that a large swan had arrived on the bents seaward of that village, and was there challenging all passers-by and especially agitating the local dogs. Didn't I think that I ought to come along and look at it? Perhaps take it away?

By this time I was agog to see this phenomenon; but taking it anywhere was a very different matter, as I indicated in no uncertain tones. However, I agreed to bend my daily steps in that direction.

I had no difficulty in finding my objective. I heard the barking, on a easterly breeze, soon after I reached the cliffs flanking Gullane Bay. Gullane is a great place for dogs. Expensive households do go in for dogs in a big way; the more expensive, the more dogs – and Gullane of course is notable for the financial tone of its residents. The canine rearguard, as it were, began to be noticeable whenever I reached the level bents area; there were the elderly, the staid and the ordinary run-of-the-mill cowards. These mainly just sat, with their tongues out. The next layer circled and eddied, but kept a judicious distance, pretending to find all sorts of interesting smells in the by-going, though keeping fairly consistent eyes on the centre of attraction. Tess, after a shrewd survey of the situation, elected to join these well-bred labradors, spaniels and dalmatians. It was the inner circle that was making the noise – all the terriers, scotties, boxers, and the very few mongrels that Gullane supports. These were extremely active in a variety of ways, rushing to and fro, rushing in and out, fangs bared – but never going anywhere actually within range of a long coiling neck, of course – and generally making the welkin ring. In the epicentre, the vortex of all this, surrounded, but with plenty of living-space, the swan paced and plodded at will, nibbling at the grass, preening the occasional feather, casually investigating the odd cigarette-end or scrap of paper. To complete the scene, one or two unhappy-looking lady dog-owners drifted in a peripheral fashion well out, making coaxing, pleading noises.

My own businesslike arrival was patently a great relief to all concerned – except to the swan, that is, who couldn't have cared less, obviously. The front-rank heroes saw this as a well-earned release from the heat and burden of the fray, and slipped back promptly into the support line; the dignified hounds perceived that there were indeed many more interesting things to be enquired into in sundry directions, this sunny morning; and the outer-edgers just packed up and went home. Tess, rather self-consciously, picked a not very convincing fight with the smallest dog that she could find. The ladies were able to relax their soft-hearted anxiety for anything that might befall four-footed animals, to undivided and unconcerned interest in the fate of a mere man.

Thus I found myself facing that swan alone – quite alone. I would dearly love at this stage, both as vital male and professional story-teller, to report really dramatic action such as the situation warranted. Unfortunately there are witnesses still extant – for it was not so very long ago. Consequently I am restricted to telling the truth – anti-climax though it is. Mind you, I was sensible, judicial, thoroughly practical. I walked around the bird – as close at least as some of the dogs had done – and inspected it from most angles. I assured myself that it was a mute, almost too fully grown, probably a male, in excellent physical condition, with no signs of injury to wings – and clearly none to legs. Whether it was an ordinary wild bird – or an extraordinary one, rather – with ambitions, or merely a semi-tame specimen escaped from some park or pond, there was no means of knowing. No ring or other marking showed on it, at any rate. It seemed to be in good order, perfectly happy – and obviously quite well able to look after itself. What was there for me to do? For anybody to do? Nothing – decidedly nothing. It is still a free country, isn't it?

As though to substantiate my essentially reasonable view of the entire situation, the creature presently demonstrated that it was certainly where it was of its own volition. Having ignored me entirely from the first, it suddenly stretched its great wings, made a little tip-toed run, and took off. The wind of its going fanned my face. Admittedly it did not fly very far, as mileage went, contenting itself with beating off for some hundreds of yards, in a leisurely way, then turning back in a wide circle and wheeling round the area a few times on musically-droning wings, before planing down to settle again in almost precisely the same spot from which it had risen. Presumably it was merely taking a little exercise.

I looked hard all around me, to underline the justification of my entire attitude, before striding purposefully away – Tess well in the lead.

I agree that there ought really to be some point to this long and so apparently unfinished epic – some sequel, at least. There may well have been, too; but if so it did not occur within the scope of my knowledge or information – or perhaps within economical 'phoning distance of Aberlady. I had a discreet look back in the same vicinity next day, and the swan was gone, without trace. Nor have I heard it so much as mentioned since – save by my wife. And she, of course has a thing about swans.

CHAPTER NINE

In Search of Jovey Gray

I have frequently mentioned Jovey's Neuk – properly that little sandy cove immediately to the west of the Pulpit Rock at Gullane Point, but more commonly accepted by the local people to describe the entire sand-hill area. Even in this small matter of nomenclature, however, my strange enchanted tract is as topsy-turvy and extraordinary as in almost every other aspect. For by local people I mean the inhabitants of Aberlady only – and not Gullane. In Gullane, I have found, few residents know what I mean when I talk about Jovey's Neuk. It never seems to be called that, there. Not that it is called anything at all, by most – for here also it is *terra incognita* to all save a very

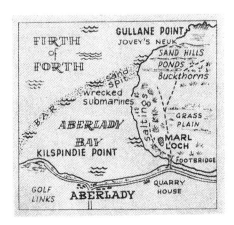

few, strangely enough, a place beyond the ken of douce and respectable folk. And, of course, there are no folk more respectable than those of Gullane. When it is referred to at all, my territory seems to be called just The Point, or 'out beyond The Point' or 'the bents beyond the Fourteenth Hole' – of Gullane No 1 Course, needless to say. Yet Gullane is situated much nearer the area in question – only a mile or so away

indeed, to Aberlady's three, and lacking the great barrier of the Bay in between. In Aberlady, of course, the place is never called Gullane Point – always Jovey's Neuk, or just 'oot ayont the Brig'. Just to add to the confusion, some maps spell the spot Jophie's Neuk.

Now this intrigues me, quite foolishly perhaps. I seem to discern all sorts of subtle influences at work here, a deep and hidden dichotomy. Or not really hidden, perhaps, for the two villages are as different as chalk from cheese in almost every respect – quite astonishingly so. Aberlady is much more authentically an ancient East Lothian village, traditional, unchanging, with a great many of its families having their roots there for uncounted generations. Sandwiched between its two large landed estates, which have remained in the same ownership for centuries, it has retained something of the feudal and clannish atmosphere into which newcomers are not absorbed very readily. It is the capital of its own wide parish, with quite a resounding history – and was once the port of Haddington, and so might claim to have been the second most important place in the county. It has the inevitable new council housing scheme, but this is tucked away round the back of the village and does not obtrude. Otherwise most of the houses are old, of local sandstone with red pan-tiled roofs. The majority of its people work locally, only a comparatively small proportion commuting daily to Edinburgh.

Gullane is quite the reverse to all this. Though much larger, it gives the impression of being much newer. This is not really true, for Gullane or Goolan or Golyn was an ancient village and parish also. But it lost its parish status as far back as the early 17th century when King Jamie Saxt deposed its vicar for the filthy and detestable sin of smoking tobacco, and removed its church to Dirleton, the next village two miles further to the east. It has won its church back since then, but never its parochial standing. Nevertheless, the ruins of the ancient Kirk of St Andrew, Gullane, dedicated in the 12th century – and

therefore in fact much older than Aberlady Kirk, indeed one
of the oldest churches in Scotland – still stand, with their
Norman chancel arch, in the kirkyard. Moreover the Goose
Green of Gullane is as old-world and authentic a village green
as is to be found in the length and breadth of the land,
although, reversing Aberlady's tactics, this delightful amenity
is not to be seen from the modern main street through which

the road runs. But by and large Gullane is a modern place, its
new houses vastly outnumbering the old – and expensive ones
outnumbering the other kind – its traditions of much more
recent origin and very largely connected with the game of golf.
Completely ringed with golf courses instead of ancient
demesnes – Muirfield, Gullane Numbers One, Two and Three,
and Luffness – this is scarcely to be wondered at. With its
excellent bathing beach contributing, it has become a most

popular place in consequence, for prosperous folk to live, within a convenient distance of the capital city for businessfolk, and for others to retire to, especially from the upper ranks of the services, and so on. I have heard it described by an old Aberlady resident as 'nae mair'n a bluidy stuck-up doarmitory suburb' – but that perhaps is unkind and prejudiced. Money admittedly does talk with a much louder voice in Gullane than in its neighbouring village, and inevitably the accent is more Anglified than Doric. In this connection it is recorded that there are three distinct occupation layers in Gullane, and each gives the village a different name. Those on the Hill – that is those whose houses occupy the higher and more desirable sites – plus those who would like to be taken as living there, refer to it as Gillan; those further down, along the main street and near the shops, call it Gullan; while the small and diminishing residue of the original indigenous population, tucked away in odd corners, still pronounce it by the ancient name of Goolan. These last, I fear, are fighting a losing battle. Sad to admit, I myself say Gillan oftener than I remember to say Goolan. Yet how this now almost obligatory Gillan pronunciation came about I do not know. At the beginning of the Second World War when, in the optimistic hope of completely misleading the anticipated German invaders, all local signposts were banished on stern orders from Westminster, one pointing east at the Wynd in Aberlady read: 'To Gulan 2 miles'. Which would seem to indicate the authentic pronunciation.

Perhaps this digression may be forgiven me if it helps to reveal why Aberlady talks about Jovey's Neuk – without ever going there – and Gullane refers to it as The Point, or The Bents, with equal lack of physical contact.

The semi-legendary Jovey Gray from whom the cove took its name, despite my enquiries and probings, remains typically difficult to pin down and docket – which is as it should be,

97

undoubtedly. It seems to be accepted that he was the resident caretaker of the presumably only intermittently-worked iron-stone mine at the Point, the slag-heaps of which are still to be discerned. When he flourished is highly debatable; in a diary written by an Aberlady worthy, the admirable J P Reid, in the 1880s, 'Jova' Gray was apparently as dim and legendary a

figure as he is today. That he was a notable character seems indisputable, and that he was esteemed a hermit inevitable. If he lived alone out at this remote, exposed and altogether remarkable place, he could not be anything else.

The foundations of Jovey's tiny cottage are still to be traced when the slanting sun casts long shadows on the green turf, just a few yards back from the restless waves, midway between the Pulpit Rock and the inlet still known as Ironstone Cove. It has been a most humble dwelling of two small apartments – one no doubt to house the cow which he is reputed to have kept, and to which the mushrooms which still flourish here in the season are supposed to testify. Nearby, to the east, down at beach level, is the piped spring that he used – the same in

which the diminutive eider-chick conducted its joyful regatta – and for which I have cause to offer him up my grateful thanks each and every warm summer day, after the miles of walking. This well is strangely elusive. I know people who have been coming to Jovey's Neuk for years who have never found it. Indeed I myself, after my period of absence on war service 'lost' it and did not stumble on it again for many days. Yet there it is, plain for all to see, under a bank of ironstone tailings, an iron spout pouring a never-failing trickle of cold crystal into the little pool it has formed in the shingle. It is the only fresh water to be had on all this stretch of coast.

One of the tales about Jovey Gray is that he used to keep an eagle out here in a cage. Somehow, I have never credited this – even allowing for the usual exaggeration, and the eagle perhaps only a peregrine or other lesser falcon. I just do not believe that any man who could live so close to utter and complete freedom as did he, so much part of the untrammeled elements, alone amidst that sunsoaked dune country, at the edge of the limitless glittering sea, under the sailing cloud-galleons of great skies, the only sounds in his ears the crooning of the eiders, the trilling of the larks, and the sough and sigh of the boundless tide – no such man could or would hold a soaring eagle captive in a cage. It is not to be considered.

I have a fairly clear mind-picture of Jehovah Gray, strangely enough, despite the comprehensive vagueness of his history – however wrong I may be. Whether Jehovah was his baptismal name or a mere descriptive sobriquet we shall presumably never know – but I prefer it to be a justified nickname. I see a big, broad massive man of the old salt variety, square-built, with a leonine head of white hair and a ruddy complexion, and, curiously enough, a roving, gleaming even sarcastic eye, blue as the sea around him. Why this last, don't ask me. I see him always dressed in a fisherman's blue jersey, with his head ever bare and his silver locks streaming in the wind. I am aware of a great fellow-feeling for Jovey Gray, the supreme individualist, the self-contained and self-sufficient whole man, whose haunting of this strange and rewarding territory was so much more wholehearted, comprehensive and genuine than is my

100

own feeble infatuation. He must have known the birds and the beasts as not many know them; few can have lived closer to the elements; his life must have been full of sun and light and

movement; he must have been the beachcomber *par excellence* – and I can visualise the interior of his little cottage furnished with the very cream of years of the tides' offerings. He would live well, too, for most of the year – especially if, as is assumed, the salmon stake-nets that still can be traced were his, with wildfowl, rabbits and hares galore, flounders to be speared on the outgoing tide, rock-cod to be caught off the Point, shell-fish, even oysters in the Bay – they are still there, but said to be spoiled by sewage – wild strawberries thick on the braes behind his cottage, and mushrooms dotting the turf. Of fuel he would never run short. He must have known great peace, great challenge, great beauty, great awareness of his Creator. I just cannot see that eagle in a cage.

Today the green woodpecker haunts the site of his house. It is always thereabouts that I see it – one single, lone bird that presumably is not lonely, far from its natural habitat with not a tree to peck. Sometimes I wonder . . . ?

A hundred yards, perhaps, to the west of the cottage site, the Pulpit Rock, sometimes called The Old Man, thrusts out at the very extremity of Gullane Point – or did thrust, I should say. This is one of the major mysteries of the place. Until about three years ago this rock rose at the tip of the rocky peninsula like an upstanding wart on a fine nose, shaped exactly like a pulpit. For untold centuries it was there, a kenspeckle and well-known landmark. Then, one summer morning, it was gone. Just like that. Entirely disappeared, as though sheared off at the base by some giant saw. There had been no storm. No blasting had been heard; anyway, it is almost inconceivable that anyone should have deliberately carted the necessary blasting apparatus all the way out here – it would have to have been done by tractor and trailer – for the extraordinary purpose of getting rid of the Pulpit Rock. Moreover there was no sign of it, or of its debris, on the firm sand directly beneath, on to which it would have to have fallen. Admittedly the tide could wash away traces of activity, but not great sections of boulder. Nor were any fragments to be discovered scattered about the rocks on either side. This was the greatest mystery of all. The thing, after all, was over four feet high and of equal girth, a great cube of very solid rock that must have weighed tons. To disappear like that without trace! People still ask me where it is, what happened to it? And I can only refer them to the late Jehovah Gray and possibly the green woodpecker. Perhaps that pulpit, like the other that was removed from nearby Gullane Kirk in the 17th century, was being somehow misused, defiled, of a summer's night. With something more potent than tobacco smoke. East Lothian, after all, as King Jamie was at pains to prove, was ever the headquarters and nerve-centre of witchcraft, warlockry and the black arts. North Berwick's pulpit, it will be recollected, was the Devil's principal rostrum in Scotland. Enchantment may not be so far out, as descriptive of this fair corner of the land.

On the subject of dark doings, there used to be considerable scope for deep and abysmal exploration here at Gullane Point, now, happily or otherwise, precluded. The old workings of the ironstone mine used to be a magnet for the more adventurous youth of the district, who came out here with candles, screwed-up courage and capacious pockets. Fifty yards or so behind Jovey's cottage there is a little bluff of naked rock, and at the foot of this, now blocked up with debris and rubbish, was the entrance to the mine. When first I came to Aberlady, the gap was still perhaps eighteen inches high. Now it is not to be seen – although Tess still finds its position fascinating, seldom failing to sniff here amongst the litter ecstatically, no doubt scenting the strangest of smells and imagining this to be the portals of the grandfather of all rabbit-holes, in which may well dwell quarry so exciting as indeed to preclude a discreet dog from digging a way in. Men of my own age brought up in Aberlady, however, describe how as boys, entering here was quite possible – although even then they had to crawl on their stomachs. Once inside, apparently, they were able to stand up almost at once, light their candles, and proceed.

From all accounts the workings, dug out of the stone, were fairly sound and secure, however off-putting to those with any tendency to claustrophobia. Estimates vary as to how far the tunnels and galleries extend, but all agree that there are innumerable side-alleys and arteries, indeed a frightening network of saps, adits and horrible gullets, hung with stalactites and haunted by bats – which, flapping out in a rush when disturbed, were all too apt to extinguish the precious candles. I mentioned capacious pockets; these were for filling with fine shingle from the beach so that pale gleaming trails might be dribbled along the floor to lead intrepid explorers back to safety – an eminently sensible precaution.

Of the various estimates given as to how far under Gullane Hill those mine workings go, some say hundreds of yards, some say miles – depending I gather on the imagination of the informant and his ambition to cut a heroic figure; but it seems to be generally accepted that they do penetrate a considerable distance and climb quite consistently in the process – presumably following the rising contours of the ironstone seams. Inevitably stories of smuggling have been linked with these sub-terranean passages – and I suppose that there could indeed be more far-fetched notions, for surely never was a coast within easy distance of major markets more apt for the undisturbed importation of supplies. At least I make it so, and in present-day conditions, in my novel *A Drug On The Market*. In that book I was faced with the problem of finding a suitable landing-place for small craft in the vicinity of the Point. It was the fact that somehow the ironstone barges must have had some such landing – for it is the tradition that the ore was all transported by sea – that led me to what I believe to be the solution. To Jovey's actual Neuk, in fact. Why was it called Jovey's Neuk if it had not some especial significance? Ironstone Cove is in fact closer to both the cottage and the mine – but no boats could land there because of the screen of reefs and skerries off-shore. That applies everywhere round the rocky headland – except off the Neuk itself. Farther to the west the open sandy beach shelves much too slowly for anything with greater draught than a canoe to make a landing. But the Neuk has a somewhat deeper approach, protected on either side by breakwaters of rock. Here boats *could* be sailed in and run up on to the smooth beach when the tide is in. I believe this was how it was done. It is what I make to happen in my story. And two years ago a yachtsman did just this – sailed his craft in here at high tide, ran it up the strand, propped it up with posts, and spent two or three days thus, before sailing away again.

I was told by an old man, now long dead, that there was in fact a rusty iron ring set into the rocks somewhere at the Neuk, to which the ore boats were tied. I have never managed to find this. Its discovery could prove or disprove my theory.

The Point is beloved of the bird-watching fraternity – by

those who can walk, that is. For, whisper it, an ever-increasing company seem to find adequate satisfaction and scope from merely sitting in their cars in the little car park at the landward end of the footbridge, or along the roadside where it flanks the Peffer Burn, and doing their watching through binoculars from there. These I cannot believe to be the genuine article, however, for true ornithologists are tough characters in my experience. Like the wildfowlers whom they so unanimously deplore, they have to be if they are going to sit or lie for long hours in cold and exposed places, inactive, waiting upon the vagaries of rare and unco-operative birds. They perhaps may be forgiven – some proportion of them – for dressing up like Arctic explorers in anoraks, parkas, windproof trousers, mitts, rucksacks and the like, often, strangely enough, vividly coloured – which can hardly help to camouflage their presence from the astonished fowl. I may say that these more exotic examples seldom get as far as Jovey's Neuk since a minimum of five to six miles is involved, there and back. Which probably suits all concerned.

That the experts and the cognoscenti find Gullane Point a magnet is not to be wondered at, for it seems to be equally a magnet for rare birds of almost every sort. Particularly is it a focal point, seemingly, in the annual migrations and a sort of staging place in passage. In an interesting booklet fairly recently published by two prominent members of the Scottish Ornithologists' Club on the birds of the Aberlady Bay Nature Reserve, the authors declare that they have acceptable records of no fewer than 190 species and seven sub-species seen in the Bay, and from their references, a large proportion of these were observed at the Point itself. Almost every kind of diver, grebe, gull, duck, goose, hawk, wader, owl, song-bird and finch has been seen out here, including such unusual items as the white-billed diver, manx shearwater, long-tailed duck, smew, whimbrel, purple sandpiper, avocet, grey phalarope, arctic and pomarine skua, black tern, razorbill, wryneck, redwing, bluethroat, pied flycatcher, and many others. For myself, I am much too ignorant to recognise any large proportion of these, I fear – but that does not spoil my delight in knowing that they are apt to be there.

It seems strange to me that this odd promontory jutting out into the Firth should be so popular with the feathered creation, for a more exposed spot with less cover and presumably feeding facilities – save for the fish-eaters – would be hard to find. Although perhaps this only further exposes my ignorance of the subject? I cannot think that the innumerable little heaps of broken shells that lie beside isolated stones dotted all over the area, anvils for busy beaks extracting limpets, winkles, sea-slugs and the like from their coverings, in fact indicates any major attraction for a large number of species. The wrack of the tideline, of course, with its teeming life of hoppers, sea-slaters and minute crustaceans obviously draws its own large numbers of certain species; but there is nothing unique about this – the same would surely apply on practically every long sandy beach in the land.

Can it be that enchantment indeed operates on a much wider front than I had imagined, and that the fowls of the air are no more impervious than some of the rest of us?

CHAPTER TEN

Fires and Follies

There is an ever-recurring menace to my enchanted territory over the footbridge, or at least to the sand-hills area of it, that worries, infuriates and depresses me. That is the danger of fire. At first glance this might seem a strange and unlikely hazard for such a place, but it is far from that. Each year, and not only in the summer season, fires rage out here, and do great damage – a much greater damage than is evident on the surface, as it were, alarming as these conflagrations appear at the time.

Marram grass and bents are, in fact, highly susceptible to fire. Growing out of dry sand, there is presumably less moisture in their composition than in most herbage. The dead and faded last season's grasses, even after a wet winter, are extraordinarily dry and provide a highly combustible mat out of which the new season's green shoots sprout. Once fire gets a hold of this base layer, it sweeps on hungrily. And the havoc created is incalculable, in blackened desolation and unsightliness, in the death of small animals and nesting birds, in the destruction of valuable cover and shelter. But that is not the worst of it; the marram grass roots bind the sand-hills and hold the loose shifting sands in position. Once the grass is burned away, even though the roots themselves are not always wholly destroyed, the wind soon gets the sand moving again, and an established area reverts to desert once more with extraordinary speed, the wind either eroding the roots right

107

away or else burying them deep in new-blown soft sand. As in forestry, the carelessness of a moment may destroy the patient development of many years.

This last winter, for instance, a wide swathe of the dune country has been devastated, perhaps fifty to seventy acres running inland from the beach for hundreds of yards, leaving only absolutely bald and blackened sand behind. The winds have already been busy gouging and scouring and over-laying. That entire swathe will never be the same again.

I said that this matter infuriates and depresses as well as worries me. For it seems to show too many of my fellow-men in a very poor light indeed – and that is a grievous thing. It is not so much the actual starting of the fires that upsets me – frequently they are the result of mere thoughtlessness. Usually they arise from badly-sited picnic fires which visitors build, not out on the open beach where they would be perfectly safe, but in amongst the sand-hills themselves. I can forgive that. As I can the carelessly thrown down cigarette-end which, landing in the aforementioned mat of dead grass and fanned by the breeze, can all too quickly turn into an inferno. What really gets me down is the attitude of people responsible once the fire has started – and when I say people, I intend the indict-ment to be as comprehensive as it sounds, for it is by no means always, or usually, children who are involved. Each summer season I personally have to extinguish anything up to a dozen fires – usually single-handed. And therein lies my fury and ire. Over many many years I can recollect only two occasions where the people responsible aided me in putting out the blazes that they had started.

From my experience I know now that the immediate reac-tion of nine out of ten picnic parties or others, when they discover that their fires have set the surrounding bents alight, is to make tracks forthwith out of the area, to get as far away as possible, so as not to seem to be connected in any way with the resultant conflagration. The remaining ten per cent will accept some measure of responsibility but – and this almost equally depresses me – how utterly and appallingly feeble and misguided are their efforts in almost every case. It is a fact that seems never to occur to the incendiaries that they have to hand, and in inexhaustible quantities, all they require for putting down the flames – sand.

At an early stage such fires can be doused in only a minute or two with handfuls of loose sand thrown upon them. One would imagine that this would be self-evident – but no. I have seen parties of adults actually running to and from the tideline a hundred and more yards from the fire, in extreme agitation, with cups – yes, teacups – of seawater to toss on the merrily leaping flames, when all around them were tons and tons of sand which could have smothered the blaze with a minimum of effort and before the thing had got a grip.

Once the fire has caught hold of the grass bed, of course, it spreads outwards rapidly and comprehensively, especially if, as is usual here, a wind is blowing. Few folk, I find, at this stage, make any attempt to do anything about it. And yet, using just a little intelligence and a deal of energy, it is quite possible for even one man to get the better of a widespread blaze – as I have had to prove many times each season. Grass fires, by their very nature, although fast-moving, have little substance to them, and beating with a flat driftwood board, or other object, or even stamping with the feet, can very quickly halt the advance, so long as it is done methodically, making sure that no glowing patches are left behind to flare up again. And done at the advancing edge of the blaze, however unpleasant the smoke. One would assume that it would be quite unnecessary to stress this last – but in fact helpers whom I have managed to enlist on many occasions do not seem to perceive it, and waste their time and efforts in haphazard flapping all over the place – even in the middle of it all. It is easy enough to recognise in which direction is the fire's advance; the essence of the thing is to halt this – the rest can be dealt with later, or left to burn itself out.

Perhaps I should not allow myself to get so angry as I do over this matter. Fire, the ages-old good servant and terrible master of mankind, once it gets out of hand, seems consistently to paralyse the intelligence and wits of otherwise sensible folk. The sight and sound and smell of it seems to have the most shattering effects on morale. But surely those who discover and reach a territory like this – that is, not the great uncaring multitude, but those who obviously must love privacy rather than crowds, the quiet and distant places rather than mass entertainment, who must come here for beauty and peace, and who must be at the least fair walkers and of some vigour of body and mind to reach the place at all – surely these could be expected to react more satisfactorily to this challenge?

Let it not be thought that I am one of those single-minded conservationists, a thou-shalt-notter, or any sort of spoilsport. I recognise that it takes every kind to make a world, and that none of us is perfect, and that my likes and dislikes should set no standard for other folk. I am not even against picnic fires out here – although they are in fact forbidden by the Nature Reserve by-laws – agreeing wholeheartedly that a picnic is not the same thing at all without a fire, and the presence of so much driftwood an almost irresistible invitation. But some elementary forethought is surely prescriptive upon all who light fires in the open, whether in a public or a private place? Why, oh why should it be considered almost *de rigueur*, apparently, for picnic parties, as the last thing to be done before they pack up and leave, to pile all the collected and unburned fuel on the fire – presumably as a sort of assurance that none of their timber-collecting efforts should be wasted? With all the combustible material here available, this in most cases means that for half-an-hour or so after the party has departed, a sizeable bonfire is blazing and sparking unattended, larger

110

than anything that they had made when present – with frequently disastrous results. The numbers of such deserted bonfires that I put out each year is extraordinary.

Do you wonder that I wonder?

Two incidents will sufficiently illustrate my theme – and demonstrate that the fault lies not wholly with, say, irresponsible visitors from the city. One late August afternoon a year or two ago I was heading for home having just returned across Gullane Bay. I had reached the top of the cliffs at the Hummel Rock when, looking westwards across the low ground towards Jovey's Neuk, I saw two people running, a man and a woman, both middle-aged. My interest was caught, for of course it is a little unusual to see such folk running in such a place. Then I perceived the blue film of smoke rising behind them, seawards – and I began to run likewise.

We were however running in opposite directions. I towards the fire, they away from it. There was no other soul in sight. We did not pass each other nearer than perhaps 200 yards – near enough however for me to recognise this pair as Gullane residents, whom I have seen not infrequently out here but whose name I do not know. They had a greyhound with them, as always. I shouted and waved to them, pointing urgently backwards, but without acknowledgement.

At the conflagration I found ablaze an area of perhaps fifty yards diameter stemming from their still-roaring picnic fire. With Tess barking furiously I set to without pause, with a piece of three-ply boarding that I had grabbed up from the beach in passing, to beat out the advancing outer perimeter of foot-high flame. Wearing only the briefest swimming-trunks and rubber shoes, I was but ill-clad for the task, and it took a lot of hard work, much sweat and a deal of singeing before I was able at least to halt the forward spread. At this stage, peering with running eyes through the billowing smoke, I perceived the couple responsible now sitting on the top of the cliffs where I myself had first spied them, watching me, their dog beside them.

It took me fully another twenty minutes to beat that fire to a standstill, and all that time the pair sat on the cliff, about 300 yards away, and watched me. When at last, blackened, sweaty and panting, I straightened my aching back, the job done, I must confess that I so far forgot myself as to shake my fist and shout gasping incoherences in their direction. They had the grace then, at any rate, to get up and hurry off towards Gullane – whilst I headed into the inviting waves nearby for a much-needed and cooling dip.

The other incident that I will describe happened in the same locality in fact, though inland somewhat – on the rim of Gullane Golf Course itself, indeed. Once again I was heading homeward of an afternoon when I saw the pall of smoke ahead of me, and commenced to run. It was grass well alight, in the area back from the cliff-top, and it was spreading directly inland on a sea breeze, across the rough of the golf course. One small boy, in bathing-trunks like myself, stood by and stared unhappily. Here was no picnic place, and clearly it was none of the boy's doing, for he had nowhere about him to carry matches. Almost certainly this blaze was the result of a golfer's cigarette-end cast down into the rough. Far up from the beach, no convenient driftwood lay about here for beating purposes. Indeed there was nothing here to fight the fire with save our own persons. Shouting to the lad to get round to the other side of the burning area, and then to copy me, I started to jump and stamp on the outer rim of the flame, in my rubber sandshoes. There was nothing in the least heroic about this, I hasten to point out; this tussock grass is considerably shorter than the sand-hill marram grass, and the flames were no more than six inches high. But there was a deeper cover nearby for the flames to grip, and a buckthorn clump not far off.

That dancing stamping process was far from efficient – and

112

here was no loose sand to throw; but gradually we got the fire under control, my young assistant working like a Trojan. I suppose that we were the best part of an exhausting hour in achieving the desired result – and Tess was hoarse with continuous and enthusiastic but quite profitless barking. The point of this story, however, lies in the attitude of the golfers. It is a busy and popular course, and there was no lack of players that summer day passing our fire. They had to pass it, indeed. Pass is the significant word. Some paused in their passing – the majority, probably. In fact, for most of the time, the two of us had quite a gallery of interested folk watching – well to the right side of the smoke and heat, of course – even though its composition kept changing. But not one individual came to give us a hand in the fight. Some, I suppose, may have concluded that it was *our* fire, our fault, and that the two sweaty and disreputable near-naked characters could jolly well put out what they had started. But even so, after all, it was *their* golf course, the grass being burned was their rough, and the buckthorns threatened bound the sand from spreading over their fairway. Yet none . . . !

Oh, well – enough of fires, passers-by on the other side, and chips on shoulders. I fancy that I have made my point, if not indeed laboured it.

From fire to flood, from the heedless to the over-heedful. It is not only the irresponsible who can cause havoc; others by the opposite process of over-enthusiasm in well-doing can likewise upset carefully balanced natural laws, with sad results. As in the matter of the seaward, lower, track stretching from the footbridge to the dune country across the grass plain. A year or two after the setting up of the Nature Reserve, some of the more ardent young ornithologists came to the conclusion that the myriad pools of the saltings area were too small in themselves to attract the numbers of duck and waders that they would like to watch. They conceived the notion of creating

113

some larger, artificial ponds by running a number of these little pools and runnels together. To achieve this they prospected and found the outfalls of the drainage water seaward of the selected area, and thereupon dammed up these channels and flows with substantial banks of driftwood, turfs and mud, anchoring their barriers with deep-driven stakes and reinforcement against the action of high tides and floods. And, in due course they were rewarded; ponds of a sort, or at least a flooded area, began to appear to landward.

Unfortunately that was not all that was achieved. Farther inland still a vastly greater area became waterlogged, and since the lower of the two tracks to Jovey's Neuk crosses this expanse, it thereupon became all but impassable, save for those equipped with wellington-boots. It still is that way, save in the dryest weather, all but invalidating the more direct route to the sand-hills for those who have not come especially shod, and, since one does not discover this until halfway there, spoiling many an expedition for those not prepared to go the mile back to the bridge and start all over again.

What had happened, of course, was that the delicate balance of the natural drainage of a very flat area had been totally upset. The water-table here is very near to the surface, and much affected by high tides which push back the quite considerable volume of drainage-water that flows down from the high ground of Gullane Hill. Now, for many hundreds of yards inland spreads an unsavoury tract, blackened, sour and stagnant, which no self-respecting wildfowl would be seen dead in, and an age-old access to the sand-hills ruined – all with the best of intentions but perhaps a certain lack of judgement.

Nor have I noted any marked increase of duck and waders to haunt the new ponds thus created – but that may be a lack of observation on my part.

Perhaps the frogs have gained what the rest of us have lost in this. Or do frogs also shun stagnant malodorous water? At

114

any rate, they seem to be flourishing out on the grass plain these days. I fear that I am as ignorant about frogs as I am about most other things – but I am told by the knowledgeable that this curious domain is quite a special place for frogs, toads and the like, as for other subjects. So much so that one of the earnest academics concerned with the Reserve has become quite agitated at small boys fishing tadpoles in jam-jars out of the old curling pond – an activity to which small boys have been addicted since jam-jars, if not tadpoles, were invented. It seems that there are rare species of such creatures here, not to be squandered on youthful enthusiasts – although I have pointed out that the said tadpoles have well survived these depredations for many a long year before the good conservationists came along; moreover, I have noted no increase in this brand of juvenile delinquency. Also it might possibly be argued that the curling pond, if not its denisons, was made by the forefathers of these same village boys and not their betters from the city. Although that is undoubtedly rankest heresy.

Be all this as it may, there do seem to be more frogs about than I recollect a few years ago. Some days indeed, the heathlands seem to be alive with their hoppings. At others every second step along the track would seem to squelch upon the outstretched corpse of one of them. Why they suddenly die with such unanimity and great suddenness, and scattered over so wide an area, nobody has yet explained to me. I have read that frogs have soft permeable skins through which they breathe, and that contact with seawater is therefore fatal to them. It could not be that certain salt-laden winds blowing directly off the sea could thus affect them? It seems a bit far-fetched. It is strange how pathetic and appealing frogs can appear when they are stretched out dead and so very naked-looking and defenceless, whereas their pathos and appeal are, to me at least, less than obvious at other times. Or perhaps I just lack a proper appreciation of the subject.

Tess does not like frogs very much. They embarrass her. But then, a great many things embarrass Tess. She is indeed the most embarrassable dog alive – and in some ways the most embarrassing. As you shall see.

CHAPTER ELEVEN

A Canine Optimist

The trouble with Tess is that I do not think that she realises that she is a dog, at all. Her whole attitude to life seems to be based on the conviction that she is something else altogether. Just what, I have yet to discover – as, I fear, she has likewise. Other dogs, certainly, she considers beneath contempt. Cats are one of the many things that embarrass her, and are to be ignored completely in consequence. Human beings, I think, she looks on by and large as sentient creatures, approximately on her own level, but woefully handicapped and deficient in most attributes of good living, and therefore to be pitied. How often she looks at me with the deepest pity in her brown eyes, a forbearance rather than compassion perhaps, and usually allied to a sort of affectionate exasperation. My failings, as she makes most evident, are a source of perpetual wonder and distress to her, particularly where activity, fleetness of foot, sense of smell and general nous and gumption are concerned. I try her patience to the limit – not indeed that there is a lot of it to try, for she is quite the most impatient and demanding of living things that it has been my misfortune to encounter.

I sometimes I think that she conceives herself to be a sort of harpy, one of those composite and unique creations, half-woman and half-bird, sent to seduce, try and prey upon foolish and weak men – for she has many darting, bird-like qualities, trills in high-pitched excitement at every opportunity, and takes an extraordinary interest in all that goes on above her in

117

the ambient air, indeed projecting herself up into it at every
conceivable excuse, undeterred by the regularity and impact
with which she hurtles back to dull earth – a psychiatric case if
ever there was one.

Perhaps those short-eared owls, that follow her about
beyond the bridge, may have something – however much they
too embarrass her; they may sense one of their own kind gone
wrong, somehow – for Tess, I fear, despite her Labrador
pretensions, is a mouser, a larker, a very-small-birder, even an
insect-and-butterfly chaser. As I have indicated, embarrassing
as gun-dog for the President of the East Lothian Wildfowlers
Association. Save in that she never actually catches any of this
minor prey, she only requires a pair of wings and a modifica-
tion of her too vocal chords to turn into an owl herself. And
that is not the least complimentary name that I have called her,
either.

This leaping into the air business, this conviction that she
will on all occasions do better with her feet off the ground, is
of all her follies the most besetting. From which of the
innumerable strains that must make up her peculiar ancestry
comes this unshakeable belief, goodness knows. When she
goes after a mouse in the bent-grass – her favourite activity,
probably – she does it from the air, seeking to drop like a
distinctly unwieldy and solid plummet upon the perfectly
secure rodent, which of course is never there by the time that
the bombshell lands. Quite undeterred, she immediately
takes off on another rocket ascent, as though on springs,
whether in the hope of obtaining a bird's eye view of the quarry
or of petrifying the mouse with astonishment, I have not quite
been able to decide. Her hunting therefore becomes a series
of eruptions, like the stottings of an extremely bouncy ball –
only a deal less graceful – or of the capers of a jack-in-the-box
with St Vitus' Dance. Even the unlooked-for descent into one
of the innumerable little pools of saltings, which sometimes

happens in one of these caracoling progresses, though greatly startling her – for Tess hates water – never actually halts her. After the splash has subsided and she drags her dripping yellow body out, she merely casts a swift backwards and embarrassed glance at me, hoping that the unfortunate incident has not been noticed, shakes herself, and sets off immediately again at her aerobatics. Small wonder that the hares love her. To be a hare, on a sunny day in the dune country, with Tess in parabolic and vocally ecstatic pursuit, must be sheer heaven.

There is a very respectable-looking couple – from Gullane no doubt – who are apt to be seen of a weekend walking across the grass plain, exercising a huge and dignified Great Dane. This enormous creature naturally embarrasses Tess considerably. It is too large to be attacked in comfort, too prominent to be overlooked and dismissed, too much altogether. She usually manages to glimpse it from afar, promptly finds a hot mouse scent, and stots off urgently on a ninety degree course which can be calculated to ensure at least a quarter-mile gap in passage. One day recently, however, Tess was caught short. Panting after a really phenomenal high-level attack on a series of molehills, which had unhappily yielded no moles, she had just returned to me, for the moment exhausted, when rounding a large buckthorn clump, there was the Great Dane and escort only a few yards ahead. Knowing something at least of Tess's mental make-up, I realised that here was a crisis of the first magnitude.

I will say this for Tess – she did not hesitate for more than a couple of seconds on this occasion. Then, like an arrow from a bow, she took off – an upraised bow and a high-trajectory arrow. It must have been one of her most impressive flights – not far off twenty feet, I should say. Like a ballistic missile she soared from a standing start – but as happens to even the best regulated missiles, there was some slight technical hitch somewhere on this occasion. Probably the fact that she was exhausted from molehill-bashing affected her calculations. At any rate, she missed the Great Dane by some inches, impressive target as it made, sailing in fact right over its four-foot-high back with inches to spare. Presumably seeking to make the necessary correction for altitude and speed in midflight, Tess turned over in the air – but in vain. She landed a good eight feet beyond target with a resounding thud, and on her back. Somersaulting over twice with the residual momentum, she came to her feet eventually facing onward to Jovey's Neuk. Without even the regulation backward glance to me to see if she had escaped observation, she forthwith put her nose down to the track, succeeded in picking up the Great Dane's trail piping hot, and with great presence of mind set off upon it, determinedly pursuing the scent in the reverse direction and in entire safety. Soon she was no more than a small yellow streak in the distance.

The Great Dane never so much as paused in its grave pacing, turned its head or raised an eyebrow.

Passing the astounded couple, I raised my cap, said good afternoon, and hurried on, eyes glued on my pencil and notebook.

The fact is, Tess is not really a great help to a man striving to write a novel as he walks. Time and time again I decide, and state in no uncertain terms that this is the end, that I've had enough, that I am not taking the distracting, absurd and disobedient brute with me any more, in the interests of production, public peace and sanity. But always I succumb to the confident excitement with which she invariably greets my preparations for going walking, and the sheer consternation, disbelief and abysmal hurt in her brown eyes when I seek to leave her behind. Besides, it is quite pointless to do so really, for somehow or other she will manage to get out of the house thereafter sooner or later – we have four outside doors in our curious establishment – leap joyfully over all gates, walls, and other barriers, and follow me out over the bridge and on towards her enchantment and mine.

It was on one such occasion that, having been tracked down two-thirds of the way out to the sand-hills, I refused utterly to acknowledge Tess's arrival at my heels, to so much as glance in her direction, twist and turn her head as she would in wonder at my blindness – a dedicated writer with a mind far above mongrel dogs. I kept this up, to her extreme distress, until suddenly a hare came to her rescue and she was off after it in full cry and vaulting enthusiasm. What happened then was, I feel, highly illuminating as to Tess's obscure and complicated character. Nose down to the scent yet bounding like a kangaroo, she failed to notice, at first, that quite quickly two other hares had elected to join in the game. These two came in, as it were, at a tangent, and most clearly of a set purpose not to be left out, some miles of open country being available all around for them to depart in other directions. Just a few yards behind the first one they took up their positions, and maintained these, loping along with that unhurried ease which so infuriates the desperately bounding Tess. In this instance however, it was not fury which overtook her. Perfectly obvious to me was the precise moment when, raising her head, she perceived that there were in fact three hares in front of her, not one. I saw her falter, as it were in mid-air. Never was astonishment writ more clearly on any animal's whole aspect. And more than astonishment – concern, protest, offence, and the inevitable embarrassment. One hare was fair enough, but that it somehow should have become three was quite as unsuitable, obviously, as it was extraordinary. I don't suppose that Tess reasoned out in her curious mind that she had no chance of catching three hares, or that the entire procession looked quite ridiculous. But whatever processes took place in her head, she very swiftly came to a decision not to be

121

connected further with so unprecedented and off-putting an event. Coming to a skidding halt, she looked back at me, doubtfully. Then, so typically Tess, she turned without pause to the rising bank of sand at her side, sniffed at it intently, alertly, and commenced vigorously to dig a hole.

When I came up with her a few seconds later already only her hindquarters were showing, and she was getting fast down there after a purely imaginary and compensatory rabbit, in fine style. As I passed by however, the spouting of soft sand ceased for a moment, and the busily wagging tail was still; clearly she was listening, awaiting my reaction. When I produced none at all, neither halting nor commenting but moving steadily on, she eventually came after me, covered in sand, and tears in her eyes. And now she was limping, her left forepaw held high, as in dire pain. Still I ignored her – and when she grew tired of limping with the left foot, she switched to the right, holding this one up even higher, a pathetic sight. I must admit that this ambidexterity in the matter of injured paws conquered me, and I held out no longer against her blandishments, weakly quite omitting to make even the required gesture at sending her home – which would have been quite useless anyway. Happy as a sandboy again, Tess bounced around me, all well with her world.

She is a trier is Tess, as well as a trial, I will say that for her; the trouble is that her efforts are so wholly and consistently misdirected. It is not really stupidity, for she has lots of initiative – too much – and a certain type of shrewdness; her failing lies in the speed and cast-iron decision with which she comes to conclusions from which nothing will budge her – nearly always wrong conclusions unfortunately, as far as I am concerned. I have already explained her almost complete uselessness as a wildfowling gun-dog – which after all was the sole reason for her coming to Quarry House in the first place – owing to the fact that she is quite convinced that I hate and

loathe ducks and am only interested in their complete re-
moval from the district, whether she achieves that for me by
chasing them away, or I do so by shooting them down. Her
complete refusal to retrieve and fetch in to me shot duck, of
a dark night, quite her most maddening failure, stems of
course from the same hallucination; it is no lack of interest –
indeed, her speed at finding the shot fowl is probably quite
phenomenal, so much so that she is apt to be back at my side,
duck duly discovered and abandoned where it fell, usually
before I am halfway in the desired direction, and no amount
of cursing commands from me will convince her that there is
any further interest to be had out of finding that useless
bundle of feathers. 'Good riddance,' is patently her comment.
Thus she quite invalidates the usefulness of her extraordinary
powers of scent, keen eyes, acceptance of extreme cold and
discomfort, and indeed boundless enthusiasm.

I have said that Tess will not retrieve. This requires to be
qualified. There was the occasion of the rag-doll, for instance
– no occasion indeed, but a prolonged campaign. Once, when
walking with my wife along the tideline out near the sand spit,
we discovered Tess to be actually walking sedately to heel, a
thing that she is normally loth indeed to do. Unfortunately
she proved to be carrying in her mouth a most horrible object,
a large, battered and most filthy rag-doll, fully two feet in
length, arms stretched wide at right-angles, one-eyed, leering
as to expression, with stuffing projecting in the most unsuitable places. This highly-scented hideosity she clearly intended
to take home, contrary to her normal refusal to carry anything.
She would neither give it up nor lay it down, and it took a deal
of commanding, threatening, pleading and cajoling before
she could be parted from her treasure.

That, of course, was only the beginning. Thereafter for days
I was positively haunted by this revolting doll. Each day it had
to be dealt with. I threw it away, hid it deep in buckthorns, cast

it weighted into the sea, even buried it in a sand-dune – but always, by the time that I was halfway home, there was Tess at heel again with the eyesore. Never, I vow, did I meet so many people exercising themselves over the Timber Bridge, all to stare askance at the evidently so well-trained and obedient hound trotting close to its master's heels bearing this con-founded outsize in dolls. Each day the horror got nearer to the bridge and to Quarry House. I attempted to reverse the process; having got it parted from her and hidden it, I would give it to her again the next morning in the hope that she would convey it safely back to the anonymity of the tideline. But, no – she had no interest in the thing on the outward progress, would not so much as sniff at it. Only on the return journey would she come back to it as to a long-lost brother, gently to pick it up and convey it homeward.

Eventually, one morning, I took a box of matches with me, and burned the grinning incubus on the open sand only a few yards from the end of the footbridge – a solution that I should certainly have thought of earlier. It being on the outward march, Tess took no more interest in the procedure than if it had been a duck in need of retrieving – and being sodden with floating fuel oil waste amongst other ill-smelling things, it burned merrily. I was watched throughout, through field-glasses, by a pair of indignant ladies in a car at the bridge-end, so blatantly breaking one of the Nature Reserve by-laws – and seldom have I felt more foolish or more guilty.

For the life of me I do not know why I should be so fond of Tess.

CHAPTER TWELVE

Diggers, Dancers and Dabblers

I mentioned Tess and the molehills. Moles have greatly proliferated out here in the Nature Reserve of recent years – as they have done elsewhere, of course. In my early days in Aberlady I do not recollect seeing a single molehill once I was over the bridge. Now they are legion – which is strange, for surely seldom was there a less satisfactory area for moles? My territory consists, after all, of two basic types of terrain – waterlogged mire and dry sand. In the one, I should have expected moles to drown, and in the other to find nothing to eat. But there they are, their mounds thrusting up wherever there is a moderately dry patch in the grass plain, their runs swelling like coiling protuberant veins wherever even the thinnest layer of turf has clothed the sand-hills, so shallow has to be their mining here – moles, of course, living on worms and grubs and insects, and, in this dry sand, these are only to be found very close to the surface. It is said, too, that the animals require a lot of drinking water, digging continually through soil being thirsty work – indeed, they are reputed to sink their own private well-shafts to tap underground sources of water; where they find any such in the dune country I do not know. They must be expert dowsers as well as most effective engineers. Equally, why their runs are not perpetually flooded, in the grass plain and meres, I fail to understand.

125

They have appeared fairly recently in large numbers round about the foundations of Jovey Gray's cottage. It is dry here, of course, although the basic rock is very near the surface. And they can go no further, unless they swim.

The mole has become a national problem. Almost everywhere they have increased enormously in the war years and since, and their hillocks litter the farmers' fields, householders' gardens, golf courses, parks, almost everywhere in these islands. I caught thirteen of them one winter in my own garden, with a trap. And when my wife protests at their activities in ruining the turf, I take a certain pleasure in pointing out that it is all the fault of her own fair sex. When moleskin coats and furs were popular, there was no plague of moles. It paid to trap and kill them, for their pelts. Now women do not wear moleskin any more – why, I cannot think, for it seems to me an attractive and light-weight fur, with a certain elegance about it – and the molecatchers have gone. It is, I am assured, as simple as that.

There are two schools of thought about the moles – one large and hostile, the other small and more friendly. Most farmers belong to the first, complaining that their pasture is ruined by the burrowing activities, the grass spoiled by the casts, and the ground frequently undermined sufficiently to endanger the hooves of their stock. Also, since a mole is known to eat five to six times its own weight in worms per day, and worms are accepted as most valuable to the soil, their very presence must be harmful. Far be it from me to declare that they are wrong. On the other hand, the second school asserts that the mole is in fact an asset, that he performs a valuable function not only in keeping down noxious grubs and so on, but in acting like a small plough, aerating the soil and bringing to the surface valuable trace elements to enrich the pasture. They point out how, from time immemorial, knowledgeable old ladies have gone out and scooped the soil of molehills to put into plant-pots so that their bulbs might flourish. Probably, as in most controversies, the truth lies somewhere in the middle; that moles in controlled numbers are a good influence, but that proliferating out of hand they become a menace.

Be that as it may, the mole itself makes a more fascinating study than perhaps most would expect. Our species seems to have evolved in Central Europe – there are allied species in Africa and North America – and slowly spread its way northwards. It is believed to have got across the Channel into England before the Ice Age, but compared with its rate of spread in these recent days, its early travels seem to have been dilatory indeed. It is said to have reached as far north as Inverness only in the 15th century. In Ireland moles are reported to be comparatively rare; in fact I know one authority who asserts that they never got there at all. The usual contention is that they are to be found here and there, but that the acid soil of Ireland, which makes the grass so green, is not to the moles' liking.

In this connection the story is told in this area of a local gamekeeper who used frequently to earn the price of a drink in the hotel bar at Dirleton, four miles away, by carrying a live mole around with him in his gamebag. He used to claim that he had this mole trained to do what he told it, and for a nip of whisky would demonstrate his prowess. The system was for him to take mole and gullible customer outside, put the creature, leg tied on a string, down on the grass at the roadside, and command it to dig – whereupon it would immediately start to burrow its way into the soil. Retrieved by the string, its owner would then take it across the road on to the famed village green of Dirleton, there to set it down again and this time forbidding it to dig. The animal would always wriggle about this way and that as though desirous of burrowing, but never actually do so – to the wonder of all beholders and the quenching of the keeper's thirst. The explanation given is

127

that Dirleton Green was in fact formed out of innumerable boatloads of earth brought as ballast from Ireland in ships coming to East Lothian for coal, and for some reason dumped here. The moles, it is contended, refuse to have anything to do with this admittedly intensely green green, because of the ground's acid content.

How much truth there may be in this tale, I have no idea – but it was told to me in all seriousness.

The mole is certainly a quite extraordinary physical specimen, possessed of relatively tremendous muscular development and compact power. The speed at which one can burrow through solid earth is quite astonishing. The feet are exactly like human hands, thrusting directly outwards at right angles from the body without arms, five-fingered with strong claws, pink palms turned outwards and backwards, the forepaws perfectly adapted for efficient scooping, the hind ones for thrusting the loosened soil behind the creature as it burrows. Extra strong collar-bones are developed, which combined with the brevity of arm and the specially curved structure of the wrist-bones together produce the most effective excavating machine known to man. The mole's eyes are rudimentary and practically useless, but its nose is highly developed. Curiously it has no external ears, but internally they are there and keen indeed. Altogether a curiosity. Moreover its teeth are notably sharp and its jaws of bulldog strength and tenacity – so that I always fear for Tess as she routs up with her snout one of the shallow moleruns in the sand, after a quarry which she can smell, hear and almost see – and which is digging away its tunnel at the other end quite as fast as Tess unearths it. As with the hares, she has never yet managed to catch a mole; but if she ever does, I fear that it may prove a tartar, for I have heard fearsome stories of moles clamping their teeth right through a dog's nose, and refusing to let go even when they are dead.

The mole's engineering ability is of a high order, its galleries showing great skill of construction and ingenuity of planning, especially in the actual nesting-mound, which consists of an upper and lower gallery communicating by means of five connecting passages, the nest itself being in the lower and larger gallery. This forms the hub of a system of radiating tunnels leading out to the foraging grounds, these roads being all so arranged as to permit of swift and easy access from any point back to the central redoubt. The Creator went to a lot of trouble with the mole – presumably for some purpose.

Few people, I have found, claim to know much about moles – but everybody will profess to be reasonably knowledgeable about their enemies the weasels.

Yet ask just a few elementary questions, and how wrong most people will prove to be on this subject. I have found it generally assumed, for instance, that the weasel is quite a sizeable animal, since it kills rabbits and hares, and will attack a dog, and on occasion even a cow, a horse, or a human being. When even a certain encyclopedia declares that it attains a length of from ten to twelve inches, and the fur changes colour in the winter so that the weasel may appear clad in a fur of uniform white, what can one expect? This, of course, is the stoat or ermine, not the weasel at all. It is perhaps not surprising therefore that the majority of people, even countrymen, do not know the difference – indeed in this area both species are indiscriminately referred to as 'wheasels'.

The true weasel, however, of which there are many in my enchanted land, is a very small creature – tiny, in fact, lighter if not actually smaller than a full-grown mole. Only half the size of the stoat, it remains brown always. Though, to tell the truth, in this part of Scotland at least, the stoats seldom really become white in winter either, usually going no more than a patchy fawnish-green colour, presumably because of insufficient snow; which is an intriguing thought also. Does the individual animal, rather than the species, respond so closely to local conditions that stoats, in areas where snow is less apt to lie than others, do not take on the white protective colouring so whole-heartedly as elsewhere? Admittedly nothing could be less satisfactorily camouflaged than a white stoat in a green or brown world. If this is so, why should the creature normally be brown at all? Wouldn't the green-fawn colour be much more efficacious for most of the year? Again, why should stoats require this special winter camouflage against snow when weasels, their close cousins, are denied it, and seem to do very well without it? All very strange.

Weasels and stoats both come into the category of embarrassments, to Tess. We are always meeting them out beyond the bridge – though many more of the former than the latter – and always Tess elects not to perceive them, even when they spring out almost under her nose. Which is probably very wise of her. The weasel is really just a tiny sinuous bundle of energy, muscle and hate, its five or six inches of body seeming long for its height, its legs short, its tail unimpressive – unlike the stoat's, which is long with a bushy black tip – its neck tall, its head flattened and spade-shaped, almost snakelike. Indeed there is something very reptilian about the weasel – though nothing slow nor crawling about its gait. It must be almost the swiftest short-legged creature in existence, and can streak across rough country like a brown flash, its feet seeming scarcely to touch the ground.

I find weasels fascinating to watch, sinners as they are. Though probably sinners are always more exciting to study than saints – as the popularity of the X rating in films would seem to indicate. I fear that a weasel can usually be relied upon grievously to interrupt the flow of my writing, for it is quite absorbing to watch one skimming and bounding over the grass plain or the sand-hills, seeming almost to perform a looping flight like the woodpecker, so brief are its connections with the terrain – then, with an abruptness that the eye can scarcely comprehend, halting absolutely, without any evident slowing-down process, into an erect position, still as a brown stump of wood, sitting up on its rump and tail, apparently able to balance thus indefinitely without the faintest flicker of movement, beady eyes unblinking. This is a favourite stance with weasels; presumably they are listening and scenting as well as looking. Then, without warning or any build-up of speed, the creature is off in fullest flight again – and woe betide most other living things that may come in its way.

It used to be a common experience to hear the dying screams of rabbits being savaged by weasels out here – they leap on the rabbits' backs, sink their teeth into the neck and cling there, sucking their victims' blood until they have had enough or their prey dies under them, when they disdainfully leave the entire carcase for less selective predators and dart off after another kill. Even foxes, scores of times their size, are not too proud to follow after the tiny weasel, to take its leavings. Nowadays, although the rabbits have all but gone, the weasels nevertheless do not seem to have diminished in numbers. Presumably they find plenty of other warm-blooded things to kill; and of course they are great egg-suckers.

The weasel's neck muscles must be on a par with those of its legs – for it is a commonplace to see one of them running along a grass path, head held high, and dangling in its tiny jaws a mouse or vole or mole as large as itself, and keeping this from trailing on the ground, short as its legs are; the strain on the upstretched neck must be enormous – but no least aspect of strain is ever apparent about these elegant killers.

Recently, during another local outbreak of myxomatosis, I had a peculiar experience. I was walking along a grass track out near the dune country, when I saw a weasel coming towards me along the path. I stopped, as I always do, for sometimes the creatures are so intent on their hunting that if one stands still they may not notice until quite close. Tess saw

131

also, and promptly disappeared off elsewhere on urgent private business.

This weasel did not seem to have seen me, did not pause in its progress. But clearly it was not hunting. Indeed it was behaving very strangely, weaving about from one side of the path to the other, and not proceeding either at any speed or with the usual alert grace of movement. Not to put too fine a point on it, if I had thought that a weasel could be drunk, this was it. Without actually stumbling, the animal looked as though it might do so at any moment. I stepped aside from the track into the longer bent grasses, and waited. The weasel came on at a sort of shambling zigzagging run, right past me. and for the first time in my life I did not see the brilliant black boot-button eyes gleaming in its head. That head indeed seemed swollen and the eye area inflamed and bare. I think that weasel was blind – and blind with an identical horrible blindness to that of the residue of the former teeming rabbit population that myxomatosis was so unpleasantly killing round about. Is this a possibility? Could the dread disease be transmitted to other species? The other day I found a dead rat out near the dunes – a most unusual occurrence, as I have indicated earlier. Its coat was scabby, quite bare in patches. Its eyes had been pecked out after death, presumably by crows or black-backed gulls, so I do not know whether or not they had shown the typical inflammation that brings on blindness. But it is an alarming thought. The first sweeping dose of myxomatosis, we were assured, affected only rabbits. This latest introduction, people say, is an 'improved version', that will kill off even those few rabbits which, surviving the first, developed some sort of resistance to it. A man recently told me that he had seen a pair of partridges wandering aimlessly about on the golf course, their heads bare of feathers and apparently unable to fly . . .

I have asked one or two normally very knowledgeable

people about this matter, and none seem to know the answer. I should like to be reassured.

Strangely enough, whilst stoats seem to be much more common than weasels in this part of the world generally – at least, I see a dozen stoats for every weasel on 'the mainland' – the reverse applies out in the Bay area.

A stoat, indeed, dwells more or less permanently on our own premises. Our garden is bounded on two sides by a tall and very ancient wall, possibly as old as the 16th century, a mellow and pleasing barrier of which we are very fond, built of the two local varieties of warm sandstone, purple-brown and golden, incorporating not a few carved pieces from the convent and church of the Carmelite Friars dinged doun at the Reformation, the original mortar mixed with oystershell pinnings, stonewort growing and glowing yellow in the crevices. Some of these crevices lead into the dark, semi-hollow interior, it being a cavity-wall, and in here the stoat dwells. I suppose that there may be more than the one of them – there may even be a family, at times; but we never see more than one at a time, and quick as these creatures are in all their movements, we do not see it for long enough to establish special identifications. It whips in and out of these holes and crevices almost too swiftly for the eye to register more than the movement itself – although sometimes we will suddenly perceive that a small alert pointed golden head and beady eyes are peering out at us, from some opening, still as the stonework itself. Next second it will be gone – although a careful scrutiny may reveal it staring from some other cranny nearby. Strangely enough, my wife, who makes a great fuss about any signs of a rat about the place, is not in the least concerned about this much more wicked killer's presence with us. Talk of stoats and weasels on occasion attacking humans, she blithely dismisses – as well she may. But rats . . . !

CHAPTER THIRTEEN

A Bay of Legends

Aberlady Bay seems always to have been one of those strange places where legends grow, a hotbed for the generation of the unusual and the curious – which itself is curious, for it has always been an empty tract, devoid of human habitation other than Jovey Gray's cottage, as far as I know. Its legendary fame goes back a very long way, indeed to those misty days at the commencement of the Christian era in this land. I have traced no earlier reference than this, although Neolithic remains have been found at the other side of Gullane Bay, and Bronze Age burials across the Bay at Kilspindie. It may well have been just as odd and kenspeckle a place in prehistoric and Roman times. I can imagine druids, for instance, finding my enchanted territory entirely to their liking.

The earliest legend that I have come across, improbably enough, links the Bay and Gullane Point with Glasgow of all places, in a roundabout fashion. The story is quite an elaborate one. It concerns a pagan princess, later to become a saint. Theneu, or Thenew, or Thanea, the daughter of Loth, King of the Southern Picts or Votadini – from whom derives the name of Lothian – seems to have been a young woman of character, determination and much rude health. She appears to have become a convert to Christianity, and being a distinct enthusiast, conceived the ambition of rivalling the Virgin Mary at least in respect of producing a virgin birth. In pursuit of this purpose, she scorned all the suitors her father found for her, and in especial a prince called Owen, whom Loth was backing strongly. To escape this worthy's attentions she fled to remote country, assumed to be the Lammermuir hills – for at this time, the capital of Lothian seems to have been, not at Edinburgh, but at or near Dunpender, now known as Traprain Law, east of Haddington and about ten miles inland from Aberlady Bay. This was round about the year 517.

Prince Owen however also was a determined character, and followed her into the hills, tracing her eventually to what has been variously described as a swineherd's or a shepherd's cottage – the latter seeming more probable. The tradition is undecided as to just what happened then – but when in due course Theneu returned to Dunpender, and alone, she was indubitably, in the gross and sceptical eyes of men, no longer a virgin.

King Loth, however great a warrior, seems to have been no great shakes as a father, for on discovering his daughter's condition, he promptly ordered her to be stoned to death. This, though sad, is interesting – for since he was backing Owen's rough wooing, it looks as though he at least believed that the shepherd was the father, rather than the prince. That there was another point of view will emerge later. For some reason or another, Loth's executioners decided upon their own interpretation of stoning to death, and took the unfortunate young woman to the top of Traprain Law instead, and pushed her over. This treatment, drastic as it was, did not have the desired effect, and probably fearing sorcery the perturbed minions decided not to take any further risks of a witch's blood actually being on their hands. Accordingly they escorted Thanea down to Aberlady Bay and out to the Point, and there placed her in a tiny open coracle and consigned her to the mercies of the sea, presumably on an ebbing tide, to go where wind and storm might take her.

The almost indestructible Thanea, however, fared better

than might have seemed probable – although, after surviving being thrown down a precipice, perhaps that is not to be wondered at. Knowing the proclivity of the Firth of Forth tides to cast up all and sundry along the east shore of Aberlady Bay, I should have expected the poor lady ignominiously to be returned thither after only a brief voyage, either afloat or drowned, along with other flotsam and jetsam. But, no – the coracle survived, and is said to have drifted north-eastwards at first, to the Isle of May, some twenty miles away in the very mouth of the Firth, and then west again, a long voyage this time, of between fifty and sixty miles up-Forth, until it finally came to rest at Culross on the Fife shore.

Here was a thriving religious community under the direction of no less a celebrity than Saint Serf. The missionaries took kindly care of the misused princess, and in due course Thanea's child was born, a fine boy despite all his mothers' hard usage, and baptised into the Christian faith by the name of Kentigern. Apart from the fame of the name, this again is interesting, for Kentigern in the Gaelic could be *ceann-tighearna*, or chief or great lord, which would hardly be applied to the bastard of a shepherd; throughout his life Kentigern was accepted to be of royal parentage on both sides. Which looks as though King Loth's Pictish wrath was founded on mistaken premises – or else that the Lady Thanea had second thoughts.

Be that as it may, Kentigern grew and prospered, beloved of all, especially of the ageing Saint Serf, who bestowed on him the pet name of Mungo, said to mean 'dear and lovable.' And Saint Mungo, of course, becoming a missionary himself in course of time, journeyed to the heathen west and the Kingdom of Strathclyde. There, on the banks of the Molindinar Burn, he founded a monastery of his own at a hamlet called Cathures. Round this community grew up *Eglais-cu*, the town of Glasgow, of which Mungo is the patron saint to this day. Mungo's prenatal hardships seem to have stood him in good

136

stead, for he became a very tough customer indeed. It is said that he had a habit of often rising in the middle of the night and rushing into the middle of the Molindinar, where he sat down in the water, whatever the season or the weather, and so remained until he had completely recited the whole of the Psalms of David.

Poor Thanea, even though she did not achieve her hoped-for virgin birth, at least achieved sainthood, for she was later canonised under the name of St Enoch, and is now immortalised in the stone and glass of Glasgow's one-time great railway station.

There is another postscript to this curious story. King Loth is said to have been shot through the heart, later, by an arrow fired by the shepherd form the Lammermuirs, in revenge for what was done to his princess love – which gives added cause for thought. He was buried at the foot of Dunpender, from which his daughter had been so ineffectively tossed, and thirteen centuries later no less an individual than Sir James Y Simpson, the discoverer of chloroform – who was also an archaeologist – sought for his grave in vain, in the vicinity of certain standing stones on the farm of Cairndinnes. A year afterwards however, only forty feet away from one of them, labourers did uncover a stone coffin and remains.

I wonder whether Mungo ever came back to Aberlady Bay? Traditionally there was a Culdee religious settlement at Aberlady.

There is a gap of almost a thousand years before the next legend that I have heard about my terrain. At this time a wild boar of exceeding ferocity, it appears, was terrorising the district, with its lair somewhere out in these empty wastes. I was always under the impression that such creatures preferred to haunt thick and woodland country rather than this sort of wide open space, though perhaps I am wrong; or it may be that in those days the area was indeed wooded, or at least scrub-covered, since, given no return of the rabbits, it looks as though the proliferating little hawthorn trees will in a few years produce a scrub woodland expanse out of the grass plain, that may be merely a return to former conditions.

At any rate, the boar seems to have been more than any mere myth, for the means of its dispatch, sword and armshield, I am told, hung in Dirleton Church until comparatively modern times. The story goes that so serious did the depredations of this creature become that really substantial measures had to be taken to remove the menace. Exhortations went forth from the authorities, promises, challenges – and eventually a sufficiently gallant champion was found in the person of a member of the family of Lethington or Levington – a property famous for its later ownership by the Maitlands, and now known as Lennoxlove, near Haddington. This Lethington was presumably either quite fearless or quite desperate, and he single-handed tackled the tusker, armed apparently with nothing more adequate than the aforementioned sword and armshield – why no spear, regulation for pig-sticking, is not explained. The tradition goes that he was eventually successful in slaying the monster by the somewhat drastic expedient of thrusting sword, arm, shield and all between the boar's ravening jaws and down its throat as it leaped upon him – which I would guess implies desperation rather than dedicated courage.

As a reward he is supposed to have been granted the lands of Saltcoats, nearby, by a grateful monarch, upon which he in due course built Saltcoats Castle, the broken shell of which still remains, clearly visible from my footbridge, from which it stands eastwards about a mile. The general aspect of the building suggests, I must admit, late 16th century construction – which is surely much too late for this exploit; although of course, there may have been an earlier building incorporated in the present ruins. Indeed this is almost certain, for as early as 1450 there was a Livingston of Saltcoats whose daughter Sophia married Walter Lindsay, son of the Earl of Crawford. So they were of some substance as a family at that time.

The Lethingtons remained long at Saltcoats, and their castle continued entire and inhabited until early last century.

Of the next legend at least there are no doubts about the date, since it is based on definite historical events in the mid-16th century. There are the skeletal relics of a number of wrecks in the Bay, other than those of the two midget submarines. Most of these are the remains of superannuated fishing-boats which here met not a sudden and disastrous end but a gentle and lingering retirement and picturesque decay – for they were deliberately left here, in carefully selected spots, weighted down with stones to prevent them from drifting about, by a previous Earl of Wemyss, to improve the view. Gradually storm and tide has reduced these to mere jagged ribs and fragments, and it is debateable whether indeed they now do enhance the wide and level prospect of the mud-flats and sands.

How many other and more genuine wrecks may lie beneath the many hundreds of acres of spreading sand is a matter for guesswork – although almost certainly there must be not a few, for the outer Bay, seawards of the bar, is a favoured spot for shipping to shelter in during an easterly gale, and I have counted as many as thirty vessels, large and small, riding it out there. If the wind had veered round suddenly from north-east to north-west, as it quite frequently does, the said area could well have become a death-trap in the days before engines and motors could save the situation.

There are probably many tales and legends of such events that I have not heard, but one tradition that appeals to me is the romantic story that there are three galleons wrecked somewhere in the Bay. Not Spanish galleons, in this instance, but French. This may well be true, for French ships were here in 1549. The occasion was the English invasion under Lord Grey during the long regency of Mary of Guise for her daughter, the child Mary Queen of Scots. In 1548, the year after the disastrous Battle of Pinkie, Grey advanced through the Lammermuirs and, having taken the castle of Yester, seized Haddington, and installed therein a garrison of 2000 infantry and 500 horse. The Queen Regent and her advisers were greatly distressed – for a fortified town held by a large English garrison within seventeen miles of Edinburgh presented an intolerable threat. So great had been the Scots losses at Pinkie, that the French-born Queen turned to France for help. As a result 6000 French soldiers reached Scotland two months later – and in return the infant Queen Mary was betrothed to the Dauphin of France, and was to be sent there forthwith for her education.

The French and Scots thereupon besieged the English in Haddington, and for two years the latter held out. Many attempts were made from England to relieve the garrison, and eventually an English fleet was sent into the Forth, to anchor off Aberlady Bay, and from there to try to bring reinforcements and supplies to beleaguered Haddington. French troops manned Luffness Castle, facing the Bay, and within a couple of hundred yards of the footbridge are still to be seen the high green banks of the earthworks which they threw up against English attacks from sea. French ships were therefore sent to harry the English vessels and no doubt it is from this situation that the galleon wrecks derive. Whether the traditional three vessels were sunk in the Bay in battle, or by storm, history does not tell. There is, so far as I know, no tradition of any major sea-fight between English and French fleets – but that is not to say that such did not occur. If battle there was, the victims presumably would be apt to sink seawards of the bar, for it would be too shallow for manoeuvring landwards of it – unless, in fact, crippled, they deliberately ran into the shallows in order to beach themselves rather than sink in deep water.

I fear that such contemplations often tend to get between me and my novels, as I walk out over the tidelands.

It is perhaps not surprising that no traces of the galleons, or other wrecks for that matter, show on the wide reaches of sand at low-water, for the Bay has silted up enormously in the last hundred or so years, and the overall level must be many feet higher. Aberlady was in fact the port of Haddington, and quite fair-sized vessels used to sail up to within a few hundred yards of the village even as late as the middle of last century, to discharge coal, load grain, and so on. A large old building in the Wynd is still called The Maltings, and was in fact the warehouse where the grain was stored preparatory to being shipped by sea. Today a rowing-boat could reach this point only at highest tide, and my own flat-bottomed 'pram' is not worth launching for about one hour's boating in twelve.

Yet the entire district used to smack of the sea, of ships and sailormen and smugglers. The charters of Haddington refer to 'the Port or Haven of Aberlady together with the house of the said burgh, situated by the said port and shore thereof, called the Town of Haddington's House, with the anchorage, monies, profits, privileges, duties and customs of a free port'. It is said that indeed Aberlady existed as a port in the reign of Alexander II, that is in the early 13th century.

Aberlady even had a pilot – and always, I should think, the port would need such. The story is told locally of one of the last pilots, one Skipper Thomson. Knowledgeable of this curious coast as he would have to be, in the end it got the better of him. One stormy night he put out into the Bay in his boat, and was never seen more. He had a wooden leg however, and in due course this alone was found, washed up on the shore. His sorrowing widow, we are told, kept this beside her bed until her dying day. Only the uncharitable, I suppose, would assert that this was not proof positive of his demise.

It is about the smuggling, of course, that the great volume of legends has sprung up. There are tales of smugglers' caches, caves, underground passages and the like, from all around the Bay. I have mentioned the stories of the use of the old ironstone workings and tunnels out at Jovey's Neuk for this purpose, and there are other similar accounts of the Kilspindie shore. That admirable local chronicler, J P Reid, whose daughter still lives in the village, has even preserved for us a peculiar verse which vividly recreates those exciting days in Aberlady.

> *'Rin doon the Wynd, Willie Crunk*
> *Flee quick this nicht, John Arnot,*
> *The Dutchmen's lichts are showing*
> *Just arrived direct frae Flushing.*
> *The coast is clear, get oot the ankers,*
> *And cheat a' the Preventive Jankers!'*

I like the sound of Willie Crunk, free trader. Dutchmen's lights still burn occasionally off Aberlady Bay, when coasters from the Netherlands shelter from the wild north-easters – but alas no independently-minded and intrepid villagers sally forth into the windy dark in consequence. In *Drug On The Market*, I do my poor best to conjure up something of that stirring atmosphere for which this coast was once notorious – but I fear that the furtive import of the foul and sinister Indian Hemp is but a poor substitute for the rousing activities of Willie Crunk and John Arnot.

As I write, a north-easter does in fact blow bitterly, wildly, and my telephone has just rung. It is the local postmaster asking me whether it is possible to see from my gate, through the blown spume and the sleet showers across the Bay, if a

142

coasting steamer is indeed lying out there off the bar. He says that the owners, from Newcastle, have just telephoned him. They received a wireless message from their skipper last night saying that he was going to run for shelter to Aberlady Bay. Since when, silence.

I went to the gate, cringing in the blast, Tess hopeful that this meant a full-scale jaunt out over the bridge, to the Point at least. A small steamer can just be distinguished, darker grey beyond the driving grey curtains of the storm, bows into the wind. That is enough for me, and the postmaster, this unpleasant morning. Hard luck, Tess!

CHAPTER FOURTEEN

Oddities, Eiders and Others

I am no botanist, unfortunately, amongst the all-too-many gaps in my knowledge, but that does not prevent me from obtaining a great deal of pleasure and satisfaction from a very real source of enchantment beyond the bridge – the wild flowers.

As might be expected from so curious and unconventional a terrain, its flora is not only varied but often unusual and highly individualistic. I have already mentioned the spiky and jagged nature of the very limited sand-hill vegetation in the dune country. The vastly more extensive grass plain and the rising ground further inland – which is sand-based also, of course, but which through long years has developed a permanent sub-soil – have their own distinctive and, I rejoice to say, highly colourful plant ecology. This attracts serious botanists from afar, and expeditions from Edinburgh University are a common occurrence in spring and early summer. There are plants here, apparently, which grow in few other parts of Scotland, and in remarkable variety considering the comparatively small extent of the area.

It is not these, however, that I can write about, in my ignorance. Only the more common and kenspeckle things that strike the untutored eye because of their colour, vivid attractiveness, or prevalence. Of such, happily, there is a great

144

abundance. Indeed there are seasons when the grass plain is almost as highly coloured as an Alpine meadow, and the inland slopes blaze with a carpet of purple and yellow so solid and so brilliant as scarcely to be believed until seen. Almost as soon as I am across the bridge, in June and July, the yellow flags greet me, the tall iris banners flaunting above their serried ranks of green pikes and spears. All the way out to the dunes their rustling legions march, flanking the pools and ditches and runnels of the saltmarsh, although they are most densely marshalled in the vicinity of the Marl Loch and the curling-pond.

The humbler marsh-marigold or kingcup, of similar colour but vastly dissimilar aspect, grows in the same places, its golden bowls open, seeming to float on the surface-water like huge buttercups. Here also flourish the spearmint and queen-of-the-meadow, both filling the air with their very different fragrance.

Contributing its own haunting incense is the wild thyme, which on the drier patches almost every footstep treads but does not crush. Vividly partnering the purple thyme is the golden birdsfoot trefoil, with pink ragged robin adding its humble contribution, and purple orchis its proud one. There is the yellow ragwort, pretty enough when in bloom but a plague for the rest of the season with its tiny clinging burrs which coat my legs by the thousand, the lilac lady's-smock, scarlet pimpernel, tiny violet, lovely grass of parnassus, and a host of others. I can but behold and rejoice, dumbly – unlike the bees, which show their appreciation by coming here in their millions so that in summer time their unending murmured praise is as steady a background of sound as is the roaring of the bar in winter.

I must make special mention of the viper's bugloss. This most handsome plant, surely one of the most stately and spectacular of wild flowers, with its large vivid blooms, red

145

when unopened and gentian-blue when fully out – but both normally appearing on the one stem – is uncommon in Scotland. Personally, like the teasel, I have seen it nowhere other than here, although no doubt it does flourish elsewhere. The experts say that it is abundant in the south of England, becoming rarer as one moves north. But on the east side of Aberlady Bay, in July and August, it is legion, and a delight. Many people ask me what it is, believing it to be some rare species of cultivated plant gone wild. I have even heard it described as more beautiful than the delphinium. Strangely enough it is a member of the lowly forget-me-not family, although it grows to a height of a couple of feet and sometimes three. Almost needless to say, its stem and leaves are spiky with jagged hairs – apparently almost a prerequisite for real success out here. My wife indeed avers that long association is gradually producing the selfsame effects in me.

Two illusions shattered in one day! This morning I saw a lark singing on the ground. It landed, trilling joyously, and kept up its song as it ran along the grassy turf, out near the sand-hills. Admittedly it soon took off again into the blue, still carolling – but my theory of ethereal joy and hallelujahs, against terrestial gloom and silence, is exploded and gone. Also, I discovered, without looking for them, two larks' nests, fairly obvious and quite close together. So that theory likewise is now untenable, that these singers at heaven's gates can somehow keep their nests hidden from mere earthly eyes. Alas for such pet notions.

Fortunately my morning was redeemed for me from complete ruination by another and less negative discovery. I stumbled on no fewer than five patches of heather growing amongst the waving grasses, real heather, in a part of the grass plain where my footsteps seldom lead me – well inland from the tideline, indeed not far from where the ground begins to rise towards Gullane Hill – and all within a few hundred yards of each other. This part is marked on old maps as the Yellow Mires – although I have never heard anyone call it that in modern times. That it was once so known – possibly on account of the prevailing glow of yellow from iris, kingcups and ragwort – is proved by the sad report of a tragedy of long ago. In July 1795, four soldiers of the regiment known as Grant's Fencibles, no doubt volunteers mobilised against the current Napoleonic invasion threat, were sentenced to be shot for mutinous conduct, and although two of them were pardoned as a result of public pressure, two were indeed shot, here in the Yellow Mires, in the presence of a large crowd summoned for the occasion. It is said that even for those times, it was considered a cruel business. Presumably the regiment was here on guard duty, for this flat and lonely area has ever been considered to be one vulnerable to invasion – as witness the Luffness fortifications in Mary of Guise's day, and the long lines of concrete dragon's-teeth that were so optimistically expected to keep out Hitler's tanks in 1940, and look like being part of the landscape hereafter for as long as concrete lasts.

But to return to the heather. Here, of course, was a major discovery. Whence came it here? The nearest natural growing heather, I suppose, will be at least a dozen miles away, in the Lammermuir Hills. Perhaps there may be a small colony of it nearer, in some remote and unfrequented spot – although the highly cultivated and fertile East Lothian landscape does not lend itself to little lost wildernesses. At any rate, there can be none growing anywhere near Aberlady Bay. For how long, then, have these little clumps, none of them more than a few feet in diameter, been here? And how were they brought?

The Bay area is almost the last place I would have looked to find heather – green, low-lying, waterlogged ground, salt-sprayed. I have seen heather growing at sea-level before, of course, and out of sand – on the southern shores of the island of Bornholm in the Baltic. But the Baltic is not a salty sea, the water indeed being almost fresh in that area; moreover the ground there is not waterlogged, and anything but green.

Did birds bring these heather seeds in their beaks, from the Lammermuirs? And is this another by-product of myxomatosis? I suppose that one must expect the effects of that fell disease to be greater, more apparent, here than almost anywhere else in Scotland, for this was renowned in the past as perhaps the most extensive rabbit-warren in the land, its thousand-odd acres yielding notably large rent. Rabbit-trapping was almost a major industry in Gullane; now there is but one lonely survivor, a rather sad figure, though a genial and twinkling-eyed little man, who must cover quite a section of the county as 'Rabbit Clearance Order Officer' or some such extraordinary title, and only occasionally surveys his ancient haunts across the Timber Bridge.

I shall have to watch these heather clumps carefully. If they flourish and spread, they could well change the entire character of my territory even more drastically than the buckthorns and the hawthorns may do.

I shall have to watch myself also, of course. I must not become stuffy, stodgy and conservative over this prospect of wholesale change. After all, one of the major enchantments of the area is that it seems to be always in a state of natural transformation, a place of perpetual transition. The coastline alters yearly, eating in here and drawing back there; whole new ranges of sand-hills develop; wind blows new deep gullies and canyons, and fills up old ones with soft sand; the spiky marram-grass lays down just enough top soil for sea-turf to follow it, and then a succession of other flora; even the Pulpit Rock spirits itself away overnight.

The process has been going on for a long time, for as far back as 1813 one Robert Sommerville, writing in an agricultural review, considered that many circumstances indicated that Aberlady Bay would be recovered from the sea within another century. This was in a comment on the plan of a Reverend David Wark, of Haddington, still a century earlier, to reclaim the Bay for agriculture by means of a long and strong bulwark of thorns and whins and suchlike built right across the bar, leaving the blown sand to do the rest. This was never in fact attempted. But Sommerville seems to have envisaged the thing coming about of its own accord, because of the rate that the Bay was then shallowing and filling up with mud and sand. I must say that I am selfishly thankful that neither of these two good souls' prognostications have come true, despite the splendid acquisition to East Lothian's farming acreage that this reclamation would have made. Though, highly likely, if the thing had come about, the whole place by now would have been turned into merely one more golf course.

Nevertheless, of course, I recollect a wise and much-travelled visitor to this area once assuring me that only in this country of all Europe would such an obvious and simple piece of land-reclamation, on a large scale, have been ignored or neglected. This same morning, two other incidents served successfully to take my mind off my novel. The first took place on the green path over the grass plain, just about quarter-of-a-mile before it reaches the sand-hills. A great fluttering and excitement in front of Tess and myself sorted itself out into an eider duck and her brood of little sooty ducklings, four of them, startled out of the long grasses at the side of the track, and hurrying along the path ahead.

Hurrying, and at breakneck speed as far as the ducklings were concerned – for they were so tiny that they could each have sat comfortably in an eggcup; this rush was only comparative, however, for the mother duck, had she travelled at more than a slow waddling walk, would have quickly outpaced them. Tess and myself, at our normal pace, would have overtaken them in a few seconds.

Tess, after one wide-eyed glance, looked away in intense embarrassment at anything so ridiculous, and when I halted, promptly found for herself a purely mythical mouse in the long grasses to go sniffing after in a diametrically opposite direction.

How those ducklings ran! Their downy diminutive wings out and flapping wildly, necks outstretched, matchstick legs going so fast as to be quite invisible, peep-peeping breathlessly, they hurtled along the grassy track, tripping disastrously over clover heads, trefoil flowers and other major hazards; indeed never were all of them on their feet at one time, so frequent were their tumbles. Their mother waddled along beside them, clucking and quacking anxiously to them, and zigzagging back and forward across the yard-wide path, more in an effort to use up her urge to hurry, I imagine, than to keep me in view always out of one apprehensive eye or the other.

I waited still, for a bit, expecting the alarmed cavalcade to turn in at one of the many obvious and convenient gaps into the secure anonymity of the flanking reeds and grasses. But no – they insisted on continuing on along the open path. I paced very slowly after them.

The faithfulness of the mother astonished me. All the late spring I had been flushing these eider ducks from their nests in the grass plain, all unwillingly. They would never let me get anywhere closer than fifty or so yards before they were up and off, in heavy flight, beating their way to safety, leaving their green-brown eggs. It is the same on the rocks and in the shallows; eiders will not allow human beings to come anywhere close to them. Yet this mother duck, terrified as she must have been, would not desert her chicks. Perhaps cruelly, to test her, I walked right up, at one point, until I was only a yard or so behind the scurrying, squeaking family. Apart from the ducklings seeking to run faster still, and therefore spending most of their time of their little noses, there was no change in their progress or direction. I would have gone on past them, but feared that the old lady might die of shock. There was also Tess, lurking in the high flanking reeds, only the tip of her tail betraying her, to consider. So I dropped back again, intrigued, to watch the outcome.

All that long quarter-mile to the sand-hills, they scuttered and scrambled and squeaked. Their miniature legs – and throats – must have been quite exhausted. It became apparent that I had blundered on a really big day in the life of this family – the day that they finally left the nest and the land for the sea. Nothing was going to stop them from fulfilling that programme, either, panic-stricken as all were.

I sauntered slowly behind, at perhaps a dozen yards distance, all the way, writing nothing. When they reached the soft sand, after the turf, the ducklings fell faster then ever, with nothing firm on which to base their racing feet, and with pitfalls innumerable to fall into, made by human footprints and the like, and monstrous barriers such as razor-shells to negotiate. But there was no resting, no faltering. Up and down the sliding Himalayan sand-hill slopes they struggled, keeping notably well together, round the marram-grass clumps, their peep-peeping now so hoarse and weak as to be barely audible.

I stopped at the edge of the dunes to watch the final epic traverse of the vast desert of firm sand. The tide was far out – another weary three hundred yards at least to go. But straight as an arrow, without pause, they tackled it, until presently the little black fluffs were lost to my sight and only the waddling brown mother could be picked out against the beckoning white line of the creaming tide.

I wonder what the small fugitives-cum-explorers thought of those curling breakers when they discovered them barring their further flight?

151

We must all admire true courage, resolution, faith in a cause, when we see it, especially when frantically panic-stricken hearts are involved. I saluted that eider family. But I wondered where the drake was? No doubt far out on the bosom of the sea, amongst his crooning cronies, head tucked under his wing, fast asleep, uncaring. Alas for the whole race of fathers!

I have established, by the way, that eider drakes do croon, just as do the ducks. I watched a large colony of them, all black and white drakes, the other day, about one hundred yards off shore, with not a duck near, swaying rhythmically, drowsily, to the lift of the tide, all crooning like the answer to an insomniac's prayer. I felt my own eyelids droop as I watched and listened.

My second item of distraction was less comprehensible, less obviously epic at first sight – but perhaps with its own lesson somewhere? From the place where the dunes tail off to the sand spit, where the lower path reaches the beach, there is the best part of a mile of golden strand, stretching to Jovey's Neuk and Gullane Point, haunt of the turnstone, the oyster-catcher and the ringed plover. This is backed by the serried ranges of the sand-hills, and as I proceeded eastwards along the little path which tops the outermost ridge, seeking to shepherd my mind back to the scandalous ongoings of the 16th century, I saw that today the waders and I had not the seaboard to ourselves. Down there on the hard wet sand, along the tide's edge, a man was running.

He seemed to be a little spindly elderly man, white-haired, and somewhat blue of body – for despite the bitingly cold north-easterly wind that was blowing straight down from Spitzbergen, he was clad only in the briefest pair of bathing-trunks. He was running away from me, towards the Neuk, bent almost double, fist clenched, the picture of either determination or desperation – a brave and lonely figure.

Then as he passed approximately the halfway mark, between sand spit and Neuk, I perceived that he was not in fact alone; a little white fat dog sat solitary and small on the sand at that spot, watching him fixedly. As he came level it raised its snout into the air and howled, briefly. The runner went by without a glance, apparently, with no slackening of pace – and the little dog turned to follow him with its eyes, but with them only.

Much interested, I watched this strange proceeding. When the runner reached the thrusting rocks that shelter the Neuk, without pause he circled round and came trotting back. He seemed to me to run stiffly, awkwardly, as though it came hard on his mature bones – as indeed it ought to have done. He had none of the veteran athlete's carriage about him – in fact he looked to me to be of but feeble physique, a thin and unimpressive old man, with either the Devil at his heels or the heart of a lion.

He continued to run. Passing the dog, it howled its protest once more, but made no attempt to accompany him. I imagined that it might be sitting there, left on guard over the man's clothes – but there were no clothes to be seen. I perceived as the runner passed my stance on the dunes above, that there were in fact numerous lines of bare footprints, regularly spaced, on the otherwise virgin surface of the wet sand from which the tide had receded, stretching out of sight in each direction; so he had covered this mile-long track not a few times already.

Coaxing Tess past the neighbourhood of the little dog, I walked on, pondering, and by the time that I myself had reached Jovey's Neuk, via the sand-hills path, the marathonist was not only back again, but had turned and was heading for the sand spit once more, with every appearance of acute exhaustion and misery – but no diminution of speed.

I fear that I am incurably inquisitive, and would dearly like to have asked him why on earth he was behaving so; but obviously I had the right neither to question him nor to interrupt his so notable if self-inflicted ordeal. It was too cold to hang about and watch him farther – and moreover his seemingly endless martyrdom was bringing on in myself a limp feeling of sympathetic prostration. As I rounded the headland eventually, to pass out of sight, he was still at it.

A couple of hours or so later, when I returned homewards, man and dog had gone. I wondered where, and whether he was still running. Possibly to Edinburgh, or even further away. If so, however, he would have to carry the little dog – for it was no runner, I swear.

I felt, somehow, put out. Not only was it extraordinary, but it was unsuitable. I am afraid that I always rather pride myself on my own comparative fitness – and the other day, in a sudden onset of pouring cold rain, I ran all the way back home from the sand-hills, without stopping, and did not fail to point out to my wife that my breathing at the end at least did not prevent me telling her the tale. But that was only two-and-a-half miles. This elderly gent looked, from a distance at any rate, old enough to be my father – and goodness knows how many times two-and-a-half miles he ran.

I agree that it is not to be wondered at if my rather curious area does attract to itself some rather curious folk. I suppose that I myself must be looked upon, with some justice, as one of the most curious. I remember, years ago, at about the same place where I first saw this runner, spotting the somewhat unusual sight of a lady sitting in the sea. I am well used to seeing suitably underdressed ladies sea-bathing, needless to say; but this was not in the normal bathing season, and the lady was not only fully clad but seemed almost overdressed, in navy-blue serge costume of old-fashioned proportions, plus a large straw hat. When I first noticed her, she was sitting in the shallows, dribbling water through her fingers with evident pleasure.

Somewhat bemused, I hesitated. To have walked on past her might conceivably have embarrassed a lady inclined to solitary bathing and contemplation. I did not want to spoil her day. So I withdrew into the cover of the dunes, moving a little nearer her, to await possible developments – an ungentle-manly reaction no doubt.

Presently the lady rose to her feet. She seemed smallish, dumpy, grey-haired, and wearing an unusually long skirt – the hem of which indeed never rose above the surface. She waded slowly along, parallel with the shore, coming closer to me, and then changed direction in a casual fashion and began to stroll out to sea. Somewhat alarmed I waited, uncertain. Fortu-nately the Jovey's Neuk beach shelves very gradually, and the swimmer has indeed quite a walk before him to get into deep water. This elderly naiad went only about fifty more yards however, and then sat down again, the water now coming well up over her neatly buttoned-up bosom. Sitting there she dabbled about a little, and then carefully abstracted hatpins, took off her hat, turned it over and over in her hands, and launched it on the wavelets. After tapping it this way and that tentatively, she eventually gave it a push and set it floating off Fifewards. She sat and watched its progress on the outgoing tide with every appearance of satisfaction. It may well have been that this hat was now out of mode, and I suppose that this was as good a way of disposing of it as any.

Nevertheless, I watched with some slight concern. If the lady proceeded to follow her hat, ought I to rush out and bring her back? She certainly gave no impression of being a suicide or in any stress of emotion – and the fact that she had survived this long and retained these garments from at least the Edwardian era seemed to indicate that she could look after herself. On the other hand, her behaviour verged on the eccentric, and I would not have liked to have stood idly by if she became much more deeply involved in hydrology.

However, presently she rose up, and to my great relief maintained a steady south-westerly course until in fact she came wading out of the shallows not far from the sand spit itself, without any backward glances at her hat – which was now low in the water and all but hull-down. Water streaming from her almost ankle-length skirt, she strolled off in the most normal manner possible, without any attempt to wring out the surplus sea, and apparently unhampered by the clinging folds of wet serge. She proved to be wearing good substantial shoes and, no doubt, no-nonsense woollen stockings likewise. I watched her head unhurriedly landwards, in the general direction of the Timber Bridge, before, much impressed, I resumed by own onward journey. Undoubtedly a woman of some character. I never saw her again.

After that, it probably amounts to anticlimax to mention the rather distinguished local resident who used to come out here

156

occasionally of a summer afternoon with his family, and went in to swim, his dignified and ample person garbed in tight but well-tailored tartan trews for wearing beneath a kilt, as is the habit of some gentlemen, and a wide-brimmed white panama hat. The sight of that panama, always worn at a correct angle, riding the waves in stately fashion, and quite far out – for he was a good swimmer – used to affect me not a little. But then, as will have been gathered, I am probably easily affected.

Then there was that other notable local character, who for a while came striding out here day after day, wet or fine, lanky black hair blowing in the breeze, a sardonic and cynical young man, if not a misanthropist, with a fleering eye and long sideburns, who spoke to none, lifted only one eyebrow to any greeting of mine, and certainly was not interested in nature study nor yet was writing a novel. Indeed I never fathomed the mystery of what brought him all the way so frequently to this deserted stretch of coastline, for I never saw him looking for anything. Then abruptly his appearances ceased. I later was informed that he had been arrested, charged and sentenced for distilling illicit spirits in the attic of his home in the village.

Perhaps he had all along been prospecting a more romantic if less convenient site for his still, out at Jovey's Neuk – where he might well have sensed some aura of fellow-feeling from old Jehovah Gray and other anonymous smugglers. He never seems to have returned; which is rather a pity, for picturesque and vigorous individualists are rare in this conforming world – although, you may well contend, not apparently in Aberlady Bay. I gather that he had had a gallant war record, but since demobilisation had marched out of step with society. So, of course, have many of the great ones of the earth. Probably he was born a century or two too late, and would have made an excellent privateer, pioneer, soldier-of-fortune, or even clan chief.

That rugged individualists are no new thing in this distinctive territory is further emphasised by my recent learning of a prime example of the species, named Sandy Gibb, who used to haunt this district long before my time. Apparently Sandy was under the impression that he was made of glass, and would frequently come to a sudden halt in his perambulations, and stand stock-still in fear of falling to pieces. He had to wait then, it seemed, for somebody to come along and give him a push, so that he could continue on his way – which must have entailed a marked degree of patience on his part when in the Jovey's Neuk area. He had a formula for his request on these distressing occasions, which ran always: 'I'll thank you for a shunt, sir.' This phrase, it seemed, became a byword in the neighbourhood.

It seems perfectly obvious, in view of all this, that I shall have to keep a very strict eye upon myself.